BEYOND THE SECRET ELEPHANTS

Also by Gareth Patterson

Cry for the Lions

Where the Lion Walked

The Lions' Legacy

Last of the Free

With My Soul Amongst Lions

Dying to be Free

Making a Killing

To Walk with Lions

The Secret Elephants

My Lion's Heart

Born to be Free

BEYOND THE SECRET ELEPHANTS

OF MYSTERIOUS RELICT HOMINOIDS AND ELUSIVE LEGENDARY ELEPHANTS

GARETH PATTERSON

First published by Tracey McDonald Publishers, 2020
Copyright © 2020 by Gareth Patterson
All rights reserved.

Cover photograph © Dirk Johnen
Pen drawings © Gareth Patterson

Contents

Foreword..01

Author's Note 03

Introduction..07

1. A Strange Story 11

2. Signs of the Elephants...17

3. Reports of Otang Sightings..25

4. A New Elephant..31

5. My First Sighting 40

6. The Otang..47

7. Chance Encounters...57

8. Meeting a Human Legend: Lyall Watson..64

9. More Otang Sightings 75

10. Self-Medicating Elephants..83

11. Missing...94

12. Still Missing...104

13. Orang Pendek...111

14. Second Sighting 117

15. Other Relict Hominoids 134

16. African Relict Hominoids 142

17. Footprints 152

18. Bigfoot 160

19. Tuli...173

20. Hazardous Encounters 183

21. The Wildfires..193

22. Solitary Grey Ghosts..205

23. Conflicting Findings...213

24. A Troubled Year 223

25. The Fires Return 230

Postscript *236*

Acknowledgements...*241*

Photographic Acknowledgements..*242*

Copyright Acknowledgements...*243*

About the Author..*244*

Get Social with Gareth...*245*

Publisher's Note...*246*

FOREWORD

An open mind is central to science.

We humans are a curious species, constantly seeking to understand ourselves, our surroundings and the other species with whom we share our world. We look, listen and sense Nature in other ways, then construct hypotheses to explain what we see, constantly testing these budding theories against new observations. And by the end of the second decade of the twenty-first century, with satellite images of every corner of every continent and after centuries of expeditions and exploration, we think we know our world pretty well.

Nevertheless, every year new discoveries are made and pushing back the frontiers of science is something every scientist hopes to do...

And yet, if you are fortunate enough to witness something truly extraordinary, the scientific establishment can become hostile. If you push those frontiers too far, it can bring controversy and ridicule. Thus, it is impressive when a renowned field researcher writes a book like *Beyond the Secret Elephants* – following in the erudite footsteps of the late Lyall Watson (who we learn was a friend of the author) by exploring beyond the fringe of fringe science. Cryptozoology, palaeoanthropology, dowsing, self-medicating elephants, glimpses of the incredible – this is a fluently written account of a journey between research that is published in peer-reviewed journals and sightings of something that most would keep quiet about for fear of ridicule.

While studying the relict population of elephants in South Africa's Knysna Forest, using every technique available from old fashioned tracking to DNA analysis, Gareth Patterson became aware of an even more extraordinary species in those same rugged forests – the Otang – a hairy bipedal human-like being, not yet recognised by science.

Some will scoff at the notion of relict hominids surviving in South Africa, just as they scoff at those who report seeing Yeti in the Himalayas, Sasquatch in North America or Orang Pendek in Sumatra. And yet it was only in 2017 that a new species of orangutan was described in Sumatra, the Tapanuli Orangutan, now numbering only 800 individuals in Batang Toru – a remote and until recently inaccessible forest. If, as well as a remote habitat, we postulate a hairy hominid with a human-like intelligence who has learned over millennia to avoid humans at all costs, perhaps it is just possible that they might elude detection except for occasional sightings – exactly the pattern that emerges in this fascinating book.

Not everyone will be convinced, and until someone finds a type specimen it will remain a controversial topic, but I urge you to keep an open mind and always ask – show me the evidence!

Ian Redmond OBE
Ambassador, UNEP Convention on Migratory Species
Chairman, Ape Alliance – www.twitter.com/4apes
Chairman, The Gorilla Organization – www.gorillas.org
Ambassador and consultant, Virtual Ecotourism – www.vEcotourism.org

AUTHOR'S NOTE

Beyond the Secret Elephants is the sequel to my 2009 book, *The Secret Elephants*. In *The Secret Elephants* I told how, although the African lion and its preservation had been the main focus of much of my adult life (with elephants being omnipresent as I attempted to protect their kind too), in 2001 circumstances steered me to undertake an independent study of a mysterious elephant population on the southern tip of Africa – the secret elephants of Knysna.

As you will read, back in 1999 the local forestry department described the Knysna elephants as a 'functionally extinct population', with only one female remaining. But, thankfully, they were wrong. My research, a combination of covering thousands of kilometres on foot, as well as undertaking two DNA censuses in conjunction with one of the world's leading conservation geneticists Dr Lori Eggert, proved that a tiny but viable Knysna elephant population exists.[1] The research showed that, without the aid of humankind, the Knysna elephants – although still a highly endangered and vulnerable population – were holding their own.

Much of the range of the free-roaming Knysna elephants was transferred from the forestry department to the custodianship of South African National Parks (SANParks) in 2005 with the creation of the Garden Route National Park. Fourteen years later in February 2019, as I was planning to write this book, SANParks Knysna incredibly announced with much media fanfare that the Knysna elephants were a 'functionally extinct population' with only one female remaining. Thankfully, this assumption was once again inaccurate. The elephants exist quietly, hidden

---

1 The results were published in 2007 and 2009.

in secret places in their enormous range of hundreds of square kilometres of dense forest and mountain fynbos.

If truth be told, because of their elusiveness and the nature of their habitat, no one knows the actual number of the elephants. To establish this would be an almost impossible task – and so the mystery of the Knysna elephant endures.

Beyond the Secret Elephants tells for the very first time the full story of my almost two-decade investigation not only into the Knysna elephants but also of my startling discovery of a much more mysterious being than the elephants – a relict hominoid known by the indigenous forest people as the 'Otang'.

Although I knew about the otang from the local people – and early on in the elephant study, I had a sighting myself – I mentioned them only very briefly in *The Secret Elephants*, focusing instead on the rediscovery of the Knysna elephants and their continued survival against all odds. I was reluctant to blur the elephants' story with that of the discovery of the otang – that is, until now.

This book is not an attempt to prove the existence of the otang. I have nothing to prove to anyone. I have simply seen and experienced what I have, and so have many others. We cannot take away what we have seen and experienced. But should you choose to disbelieve what has been seen, that is entirely your prerogative.

In this book I not infrequently use the term 'relict hominoid', but what exactly are relict hominoids?

The term was probably first coined by Russian historian, philosopher and hominoid researcher Boris Porshnev, author of the book *The Present State of the Question of Relict Hominoids* (Moscow: Viniti, 1963).

In recent years the term has become almost synonymous with the scientist Dr Jeff Meldrum. Professor of Anatomy and Anthropology at Idaho State University, Meldrum is the author of the landmark book about relict hominoids (endorsed by Jane Goodall), *Sasquatch: Legend Meets Science* (Forge Books, 2007).

He is also the editor of *The Relict Hominoid Inquiry* (RHI) which has as its objective 'to promote research and provide a refereed venue for the dissemination of scholarly peer-reviewed papers exploring and evaluating the possible existence and nature of relict hominoid species around the world'. Meldrum has been described as one of the very few scientists who approach the subject of relict hominoids in an open-minded yet critical manner.

The following is Meldrum's breakdown of the term 'relict hominoid':

'Relict' is a term finding application and usage in the biological sciences. It denotes a species that has survived from an earlier period, or in a primitive form; a remnant of a formerly widespread species that persists in an isolated area. The term 'hominoid' in a colloquial sense means human-like, from the Latin homin – human, and the Latin oid – like, resembling; similar, but different.[2]

---

2 Meldrum, D.J. (2016). Sasquatch & Other Wildmen: The Search for Relict Hominoids. *Journal of Scientific Exploration*, 30(3): 355-373.

INTRODUCTION

Now ... the dark walker came gliding into shadow ...

Beowulf

When you have seen a bipedal, hair-covered human-like being, your life changes forever.

After my first sightings I developed empathy for these beings, followed by sympathy and a sense of responsibility for them.

It is now seventeen years since my first sighting which, initially, left me deeply shocked and confused. I had seen something that, according to science, does not exist. What was it? An ancient hominoid species that has endured into the present?

After the first sighting I felt deep shock for several days. I replayed the incident in my mind. I questioned myself as to whether I had actually seen it, but I always concluded that I saw what I saw. The shock made me feel numb at times. Recently, while talking about the incident to Fransje, my girlfriend at the time, she said my shock was very visible.

A few years ago I was guiding a group of six well-educated and successful middle-aged people on one of my *Secret Elephants Forest Experiences* in the same area where I had my first sighting. They had all read *The Secret Elephants* in which I briefly mention the local indigenous people's knowledge of the mysterious beings.

We were admiring the view of a valley bordering the central Knysna forest and one of the women was peering through binoculars at an eddying pool in the river below. Suddenly she said loudly, 'Gareth, what is that?' and pointed down into the valley. We all looked and we all saw it. Approximately six to seven feet tall, a strange upright being walked away from the pool and disappeared among the rocks and boulders.

After it had gone the group turned to me and asked what they had seen. I asked them if they recalled the section in *The Secret Elephants* where I had mentioned the mysterious beings known to the local people. They all nodded.

It was then that I witnessed the effect that seeing this strange being has on people. It took us more than half an hour to reach our end destination and in that time no one uttered a word. They were all clearly in shock. When we reached our destination, our goodbyes broke the silence and then they drove away.

For many years after my first sighting, I researched the mysterious being and its existence in the place where I live and work, and I also investigated reports of the existence of not dissimilar beings elsewhere in the world.

I had other sightings, and I recorded sightings reported by indigenous people in the area; I even photographed footprints of the being. But I was in a dilemma.

On the one hand I felt that I should write about it. By letting what I had seen and learnt be known, hopefully these beings might be afforded protection in that their habitat would not be further encroached upon by humankind. In Bhutan, despite the fact that the existence of the yeti (known as *migoi* in Bhutan and strongly believed in by the local people) has not been proven, the government has had the foresight to create the Sakteng Wildlife Sanctuary specifically to protect the habitat of the *migoi*.

The second part of my dilemma – apart from risk to my reputation as an internationally known wildlife conservationist and the author of eleven books! – was that letting it be known that the being exists would attract the wrong kind of attention – people seeking them for the wrong reasons. But after thinking long and hard about this, and knowing of their elusiveness and inaccessibility, I decided to write the book.

Beyond the Secret Elephants - Audio File: Part 1

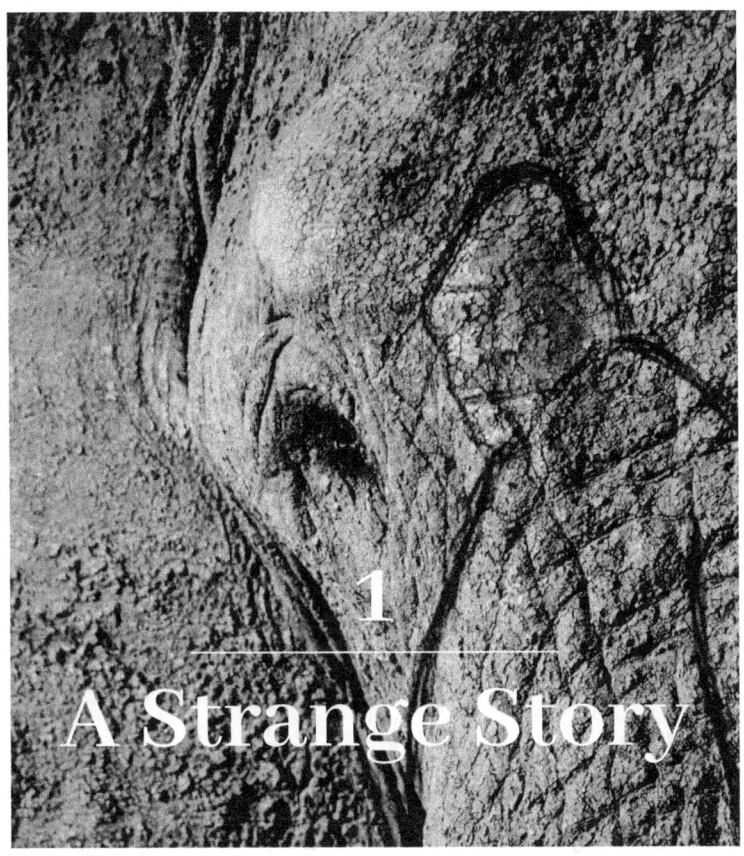

1

A Strange Story

In July 1999, at a hotel called Madiba's Tide overlooking the shimmering Knysna lagoon in the southern Cape of South Africa, I was told a strange story.

I was visiting the southern Cape with my then girlfriend, Fransje, to finalise the creation of a large natural habitat sanctuary, in partnership with the International Fund for Animal Welfare (IFAW), for a group of lions we had rescued from South Africa's sordid canned lion industry. In South Africa then, and sadly continuing today, captive-bred lions are raised to later be shot in fenced areas by international trophy hunters. In 1997, in conjunction with IFAW and the British investigative programme,

The Cook Report, we exposed to the world the horrors of canned hunting which resulted in international condemnation of the practice.

With the discussions and plans for the natural habitat sanctuary completed (the lions went on to live out the rest of their lives in the comparative freedom of the magnificent one hundred hectare sanctuary), Fransje and I decided to visit the beautiful environs of the small holiday town of Knysna for a few days – and specifically to explore the Knysna forest, home of the world's most southerly and most endangered elephants.

As I have mentioned, at the time of our visit in 1999 the local forestry authorities had reported that the Knysna elephants were now a 'functionally extinct population', claiming that only one elderly elephant remained in the expanses of the forest. They referred to this elephant as 'The Matriarch'.

For the previous two decades I had been fascinated by the elusive and extraordinary Knysna elephants on the southern tip of Africa. Now, in 1999, I had an opportunity to visit the Knysna forests for the very first time. I had vague plans that perhaps sometime in the future I should come to live in this place and learn for myself what the true status was of these legendary elephants.

For my entire adult life I have worked for the greater protection of the African lion and lived in the dry savannah and scrub lands of the lions' range. I knew nothing about the Afromontane forest that exists north of the town of Knysna.

Fransje and I were told the strange story on the morning we were about to embark into the forests for the very first time. At breakfast at Madiba's Tide the hotel manager Juan, knowing that we were about to visit the forest, sat down at our table.

Juan knew of my work with lions, having read several of my books, and he knew that I had recently investigated and exposed canned lion hunting. We had chatted the previous evening at the hotel bar and had got to know him a little. Both Fransje and I liked him.

'Gareth,' he said as he sat down, 'perhaps when the canned lion work is over, you and Fransje should move down to this beautiful place and take time off from other things to investigate what is really going on with the Knysna elephants.'

It was as though Juan had read the thoughts that had been swirling around my mind.

'The forestry department claims,' he continued, 'that there is only one lonely old female still alive, but many of us locals simply do not believe this. The forest is huge and dense. How can anyone be certain that only one elephant exists?'

Juan paused and then said, 'But if you do come down here, you must be aware that there might be a greater mystery out there than the Knysna elephants.'

Intrigued, I asked Juan to expand on this.

He gave us a wry smile and said, 'What I am about to tell you I would not have believed, had I not heard it myself. Recently I had a party of wealthy and well-travelled German guests staying at the hotel. A very nice group of people, very jovial, chatty and cheerful. An absolute pleasure having them stay with us at Madiba's Tide. Like you and Fransje, one morning they planned to drive into the forest, and before they left they asked me for directions to the central forest, which I duly gave them.'

Juan paused again before saying, 'The next time I saw my German guests was later that afternoon at the hotel bar, and they were clearly subdued and strangely quiet. Sensing something was wrong, I asked them whether everything was fine and whether they had had a good time in the forest.'

'What did they say, Juan?' asked Fransje.

Juan nodded at Fransje and said, 'It was what they saw in the forest.'

'An elephant?' Fransje ventured.

'No, Fransje,' replied Juan, 'it was beings far more mysterious than our Knysna elephants. They had followed the route I had recommended which leads up to the Diepwalle Forest Station in the central forest.'

His expression serious, Juan then said, 'The Germans told me that as they were driving towards Diepwalle they saw three upright figures on the side of the road. At first they thought they were people, but as they got closer, they realised that they were three bipedal ape-like animals which quickly crossed the road and vanished into the forest. They were russet coloured, the Germans said, and covered in hair.'

'Baboons surely, Juan?' I said.

Juan's face remained serious. 'That's what I said to them, Gareth. And then they almost got angry with me for suggesting this. These were educated, well-travelled people, and they certainly knew what baboons were. I then realised that my guests were clearly in shock because of what they had seen. They had seen something that is supposed not to have existed for hundreds of thousands of years. And they were so disturbed by what they had seen that they cut short their stay here and left first thing the next morning.'

'Extraordinary,' Fransje said, her eyes wide.

'Baboons,' I thought to myself.

Later, as we drove to the edge of the forest we came across a troop of baboons. I noticed that these Knysna baboons were quite dark and stockier than the savannah baboons I was used to. As I slowed down for us to watch the baboons, Fransje said to me, perhaps prompted by what we were watching, 'Gareth, what did you think of Juan's strange story about what his German guests saw here?'

Looking at the baboons, I paused for a moment before answering her.

Then I said, 'It certainly is a very strange story. On the one hand, as we both know, baboons will not uncommonly stand upright for short periods to get a better view of things and that must have been what the German guests saw. But ...'

'But what, Gareth?' Fransje asked.

I paused again before replying. 'Firstly, what I find strange is that, as Juan told us, the Germans were clearly in a state of shock because of what they had seen. Secondly, has Juan just fabricated or embellished the whole story? I cannot see why he would do this. He seems a genuine guy, and he knows we are not gullible tourists. The story has a hint of truth to it, but at the same time it seems totally fantastical and unbelievable.'

We continued onwards into the Knysna forest. It was like no other place I had ever seen. The forest is dense and beautiful with shafts of lemon-coloured light penetrating its depths. Moving out of the forest, we entered the big sky country of the mountain fynbos in the north. We got out of the vehicle on the top of a hill and looked around us. To the south, beyond the vastness of the dark green forest, we could just make out the Indian Ocean. To the north, as far as the eye could see, were the isolated mountain fynbos expanses.

Knowing elephants, grey ghosts even in the relatively open bush lands that I was used to, I knew that what was lying below us could conceal any number of elephants.

'There could be others out there,' I thought to myself.

And two years later, in May 2001, when Fransje and I returned to Knysna and I embarked on a full-time study, I quickly discovered that there were indeed other elephants out there.

But there were also others of another kind.

And after my first sighting of one of these beings the following year, it was I who was affected by extreme shock because of what I had seen. Like Juan's German guests, I too had seen the impossible.

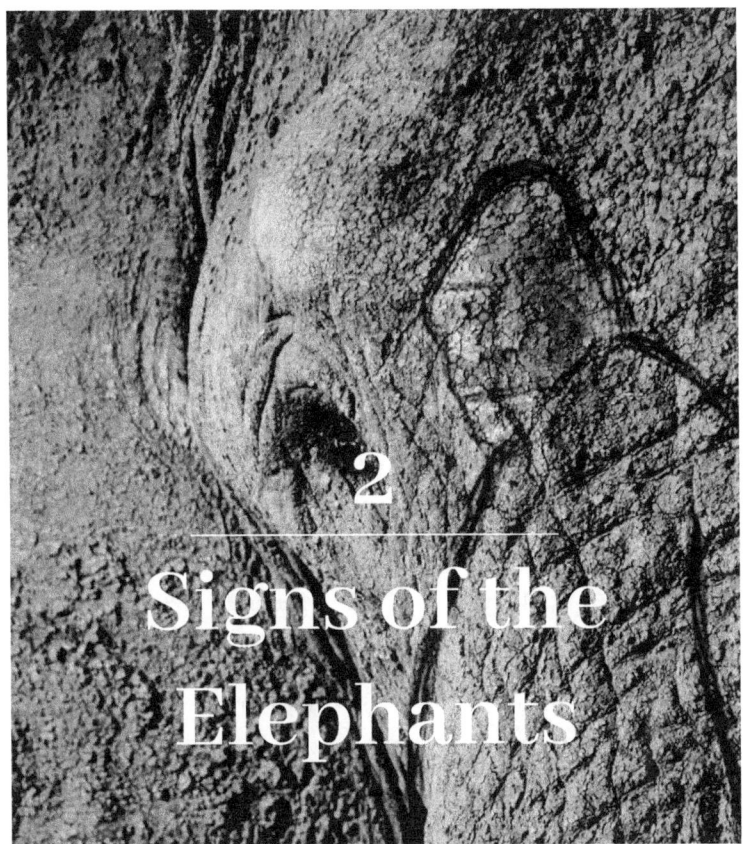

2

Signs of the Elephants

Fransje and I settled into a pine house on a hillside encircled by plantations, fynbos and patches of indigenous forest. To the south was a sweeping view down to the Knysna lagoon and to where the blue sky meets the blue waters of the Indian Ocean. To the north lay the wide expanse of the central portion of the dense and deep green Knysna forest, beyond which were the foothills of the Outeniqua Mountains.

The house was ideally situated, only seven kilometres from the town of Knysna, and literally almost a stone's throw from the edge of the central forest.

In the years to come I was to discover that the Knysna elephants ranged as close as two kilometres to where we lived, and that also we were living in the midst of the range of the mysterious beings.

In undertaking full-time research into the Knysna elephants, my baseline objectives were to try to establish the number of the elephants and the extent of their range, to learn which habitats they were utilising within that range, and to establish what their diet was.

My objective was never to physically track down the elephants on foot, see them and photograph them. This would have been stressful for the elephants. My research was non-invasive and based on respect for the animals.

Elephants in the southern Cape had been tracked and hunted down since the white man first colonised southern Africa more than 350 years ago. It has been estimated that prior to colonisation some 100 000 elephants may have existed in what is present day South Africa – with approximately 10 000 of these elephants existing in the southern Cape. By 1910 virtually the entire elephant population of the country had been wiped out by professional ivory hunters, 'sportsmen' and settler farmers. By this time only some 200 elephants remained – in four separate populations – the southern-most being the Knysna elephants.

In 1970 elephant researcher Nick Carter, who spent a year studying these elephants, estimated that only eleven or twelve existed. The persecution did not stop. Just after Carter's study, a forester working with the forestry department, in what was meant to be a clandestine killing, destroyed the most famous of the Knysna elephants – the main breeding bull Carter had named 'Adam' (and also known as 'Aftand' by the local people). The killing was uncovered, and those involved were charged, but many believed that Adam was not the only Knysna elephant to have been killed by the forestry authorities.

The Knysna elephants that I was about to study and learn about were relict survivors – descendants of victims of mass genocide.

My routine each day would be to drive out into the elephants' range and to walk for half a day learning about the Knysna elephants from the signs they left behind, such as their droppings, footprints and feeding signs – the strewn branches and leaves. It was calculated that in the first few years of the study I covered some 22 000 kilometres on foot, the equivalent of walking halfway around the world.

Early on, contrary to what had been previously claimed by the forestry authorities, I learnt that the Knysna elephants were not restricted to the dark confines of the forests, but roamed widely on the fynbos foothills of the mountains. At the commencement of my study it was thought that the 'last' remaining elephant ranged in perhaps 100 square kilometres of the central forest. Today we know that the population ranged in over 700 square kilometres of mountain fynbos, the plantations, the forest and the forest edge.

Within several weeks of starting my study it was clear to me that definitely more than one elephant existed. I was finding footprints and droppings of various sizes, indicating different individuals. By measuring the diameter of the hind footprints of elephants, their ages can be determined, and the same applies to measuring the circumference of dung balls. Early evidence was showing that the Knysna elephant population was made up of comparatively young adults. Those were uplifting times.

During the early months of the elephant study, I do not think I ever thought about the mysterious beings the German tourists claimed to have seen two years earlier. This was to change one morning when I was having a meeting with a forestry department botanical scientist at his office in Knysna. The scientist, Johan, and I had arranged to meet to identify some of the plant types the Knysna elephants were eating. Somehow during the meeting, the subject changed to the bushman paintings in the vicinity of the Knysna forest.

Then, quite unexpectedly, Johan asked me, 'Gareth, while you are out walking in the forests and the mountain fynbos, have you ever come across a type of furry upright walking ape?'

Juan's story came flooding back into my mind.

I replied that I had not and enquired why he had asked.

'I ask,' said Johan, 'because in the past couple of years we have had two separate reports from our forest workers seeing such a creature. They were absolutely shocked at the sight. The men are adamant that it walks upright and is covered in hair. I would be very interested to know what it is.'

I thought this conversation with Johan was curious. The story of the mysterious beings had arisen again, totally unprompted by me, and the subject had been brought up by a scientist who seemed to be open minded about its existence.

Thoughts about the mysterious being slipped out of my mind again in the days and weeks that followed as I began to find dramatic evidence of the Knysna elephants.

Early one grey overcast morning I was walking on a track through a pine plantation that borders an edge of the central forest when suddenly I heard a cracking sound ahead of me. I had a strong feeling that the source of the sound was elephants.

I continued onwards and at a point where the track split, one branch leading north, the other south, I found the fresh tracks of two young elephants.

The larger of the tracks was unlike any elephant footprint I had ever seen before. Instead of being etched with the usual mosaic of creases and lines, the back right footprint had an almost patchwork appearance. Immediately a name for this elephant came to mind – 'Strangefoot'.

Measuring Strangefoot's hind track and that of the second and smaller elephant, indicated that they were approximately fourteen and eight years old respectively. I named the smaller one 'The Youngster'. The fact that these were young elephants clearly illustrated that breeding had taken place in comparatively recent years, and that the Knysna elephants were a breeding population.

Continuing along the track, I soon came across a very fresh pile of droppings. The elephants had indeed been the source of the cracking sound I had heard earlier, and now they were close by. Walking onwards, I came across young trees that had been pulled to the ground and were strewn across the track. The weather was turning rapidly and the clouds had become menacingly dark.

Suddenly I heard the elephants to my right, followed by a loud crash of branches. As raindrops began to pelt down, I decided to move away. It would have been foolhardy to remain where I was, considering the conditions and my proximity to the elephants.

As I returned the way I had come, the rain began to pelt down hard and incessantly. Soon all I could hear was the rain. I had made the right decision.

Walking back through the forest to my vehicle in the pouring rain, I felt wonderfully elated by my discovery of the two young Knysna elephants.

Two weeks later I found dramatic evidence of three of these elusive elephants moving together.

Early one Sunday morning, Fransje and I set off to explore an elephant pathway that led through a pine plantation bordering on a patch of forest. We soon came across extremely fresh feeding signs and several piles of droppings. It was clear to me that this was definitely the activity of more than one elephant. It was an exciting moment.

The spoor indicated that the elephants had headed in the direction of Kom se Pad, the main track that winds through the northern section of the central forest.

We returned to our car and drove slowly along Kom se Pad. As we turned a corner we suddenly saw a mass of elephant footprints all over the road. The elephants had clearly been rushing around, moving both backwards and forwards. There were droppings on the road, as well as urine. We got out of the car to examine the fresh tracks and I quickly realised that we had come across evidence of three elephants moving together.

The tracks were small, medium, and large in size. I noticed that the medium-sized tracks were those of Strangefoot, with her distinctive patchwork pattern. I was fairly confident that the small footprints were those of The Youngster – and measurements later confirmed this. The largest footprints I had not seen before, but I suspected that they might have belonged to a young adult bull, as there appeared to be signs that perhaps mating had taken place. This would explain the presence of a young adult bull with Strangefoot and The Youngster, and the chaotic pattern of the footprints. As I looked at the signs of excited elephant activity, I said to Fransje, 'Imagine the possible birth of a baby Knysna elephant in just under two years' time!' The gestation period of elephants is twenty-two months – the longest gestation period of all mammals. Fransje grinned back at me.

We tracked the elephants along the road for about two kilometres and as we entered the edge of the forest we found the place where the elephants had climbed an embankment and headed north-east on one of their secret pathways, which was lost to us in the dense greenery.

The photographs we took that morning of the footprints on the road clearly showed the very real existence of three Knysna elephants. In the recent past, tracks of only a single Knysna elephant had been reported.

A week or so later I showed the photographs to two forest guards who had monitored elephant movements for a decade and a half, Wilfred Oraai and Karel Maswatie. They were astounded when they saw the clear evidence of three elephants. 'Good work, Gareth!' said Karel with a broad smile.

Wilfred and Karel were to become colleagues and good friends of mine in the months and years to come. Both men were totally dedicated to the Knysna elephants.

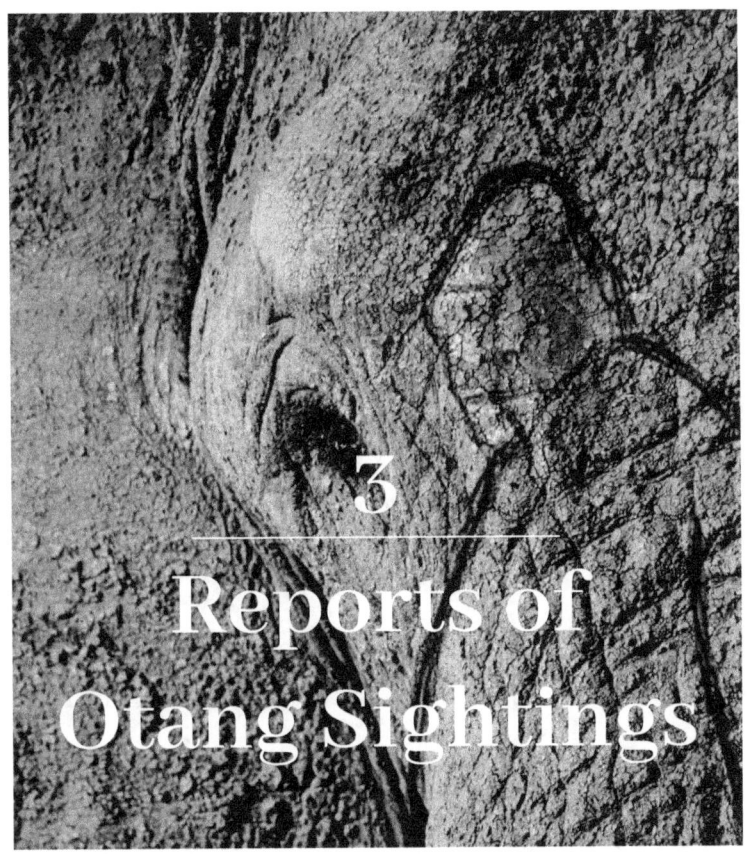

3

Reports of Otang Sightings

Incredibly, just three weeks after my discovery of three Knysna elephants moving together (and mating possibly having taken place), Wilfred and Karel were to make another dramatic discovery – the presence of a large mature bull.

On the western side of the Knysna River, beyond the dense basin of the Church Millwood forests, they sighted and even managed to film this elephant. Wilfred crept within 30 metres of where the bull was feeding on the lower slopes of the Taitskop Mountain.

Over the years I have often watched this footage and it is clear from the elephant's behaviour that he knew of Wilfred's presence, yet he showed no annoyance or fear. As Wilfred filmed, the bull raised its head to enable it to get a better view of him. This was an early indication that the Knysna elephants knew Wilfred and Karel, and soon they would begin to know me too.

At that time, and for years afterwards, it was only Wilfred, Karel, a few other forest guards and I who walked daily and extensively throughout the elephant's wide range collecting information about them. As we learnt about the elephants from the signs they left behind, such as spoor, droppings, strewn feeding signs and rubbings and scrapings on trees as they moved through the forest and fynbos, so we too were leaving behind signs. Although I was working independently of Wilfred and Karel, the three of us were leaving chemical messages behind as we walked and touched the trees.

Thinking back today, it is impossible that, with their most acute sense of smell, the elephants did not know us individually. Of this I once wrote:

> The elephants, like the guards, also leave messages, such as footprints, signs of feeding and, of course, droppings. So each day a form of information is exchanged between the elephants and the men. This could even be interpreted as a 'conversation'.

Five months into my elephant research, engrossed in my work and the remarkable findings that suggested that a viable population of Knysna elephants existed, the stories of the mysterious being were far from my mind. That was until, totally unexpectedly, like Johan's story, another account reached me.

By this time people residing in the vicinity where Fransje and I lived on the ridge overlooking the lagoon and the ocean had learnt that I was researching the elephants.

As I passed a house on my way to the forest, one of our neighbours, Albury, waved and called me over for a chat. Albury worked at the Knysna Correctional Services. He asked me how my elephant work was going and later in our conversation he remarked, 'Yes, the forest is very big, hiding the elephants as well as other strange creatures if my colleague at Correctional Services is to be believed.'

'Other strange creatures?' I said, almost sure that I knew what I was about to hear.

'Ape men,' said Albury.

He went on to tell me that his colleague had, as a child, apparently seen an 'ape man' while in a Land Rover with his brother and parents.

'We always rib him a bit when he tells this story, but he is convinced that he saw this creature, and his brother confirms what they saw. Give him a call if you would like to know more. He is a good guy, very friendly.'

Albury gave me the man's number, and I called him a few days later.

The man was indeed very friendly. 'Yes,' he said, 'Albury told me that he had a chat with you about my brother and me seeing that ape man when we were kids. Man, I will never forget that for the rest of my life. What happened was this', he continued, 'my brother and I were with my parents, taking a ride one Sunday in the hills north of the forest. We were in the old "Landie" (Land Rover), an open roof affair. We would go out in it most Sundays with the folks. Mom and Dad upfront, and me and my brother in the back.'

He paused for a while before saying, 'We were rounding a hill when both my *boet* (brother) and I saw it, covered in hair, walking on two legs and moving away into the fynbos. And then it was gone. I turned to look at my brother and his eyes were wide and his mouth was open. The strange thing was that we were speechless for a while. Shock, I guess.'

I asked him if they had told their parents what they had seen.

'Only when we got home, Gareth, and they brushed it off saying that we had seen a baboon. I have lived here my whole life and I certainly know what a baboon is, and that was no baboon. And my brother also knows what he saw. We still talk about it sometimes, all these years later.'

Before we ended our conversation, he said, 'I do not care, nor does my brother, if people do not believe what we saw. It used to hurt us a bit, but we simply do not care any more. We know what we saw, and today when we think back to that day and what we saw, we feel that it was actually a real privilege to have seen it.'

I thanked him for talking to me, put my phone down on my desk, and thought hard about what the man had told me.

Whether it was Juan's German guests, Johan's forestry workers or Albury's colleague, these all seemed to be unfabricated and almost innocent reports. Though cautiously sceptical of the existence of the mysterious beings, I could not fault how spontaneous and consistent the separate reports were, although they derived from three unrelated and diverse parties – a group of foreign tourists, people who spend their lives working in the forest, and Albury's colleague and his brother's childhood experience.

In all three reports, the experience of feeling extreme shock after seeing the creature was a commonality. And I was curious about this commonality.

I had come to Knysna to conduct research into the world's most elusive and endangered elephant population of which, it was reported, only one remained. Within the first year of research, the assumption that only one elephant remained, had (thankfully) been proved by me and by Wilfred and Karel to be wrong, but the seemingly genuine three reports of the mysterious beings had me baffled.

What had the people seen?

By now Wilfred, Karel and I were getting to know one another reasonably well and we were sharing our elephant findings, so I decided to ask the two men whether, in their long years of patrolling the forest, they had encountered such a creature.

When I asked this question, both men's normally open faces became a little evasive. If they had seen something, they were certainly not telling.

'No, Gareth, not by us,' replied Wilfred, but interestingly he then said, 'but the old people used to talk about the existence of such an animal.'

I left my questioning at that, and our conversation turned back to the elephants.

On another occasion when I was talking to Lietie Sam, a veteran forest guard, and importantly not mentioning the words 'ape men', I asked him whether he knew about any strange animals in the forest and mountain fynbos. Spontaneously, and without hesitation he replied, 'Not I myself, Gareth, but in the past the people knew of an animal here that was something like a gorilla.'

Both Wilfred and Lietie Sam's comments intrigued me. Now I seemingly had confirmation of the existence of the strange beings in the fairly recent past, as well two eyewitness accounts over the past few years – that of the Germans and the forestry workers – as well as Albury's colleague's eyewitness account that went back perhaps twenty years.

Ever the cautious sceptic, I felt that this seemed to be a fairly consistent spread of reports of the creature's existence going back decades and almost up to the present.

I found this hard to ignore but even harder to understand or explain.

Since I was there to research and study the elusive Knysna elephants, my focus once again went firmly back to them – but now a kernel of curiosity about the mysterious beings remained at the back of my mind.

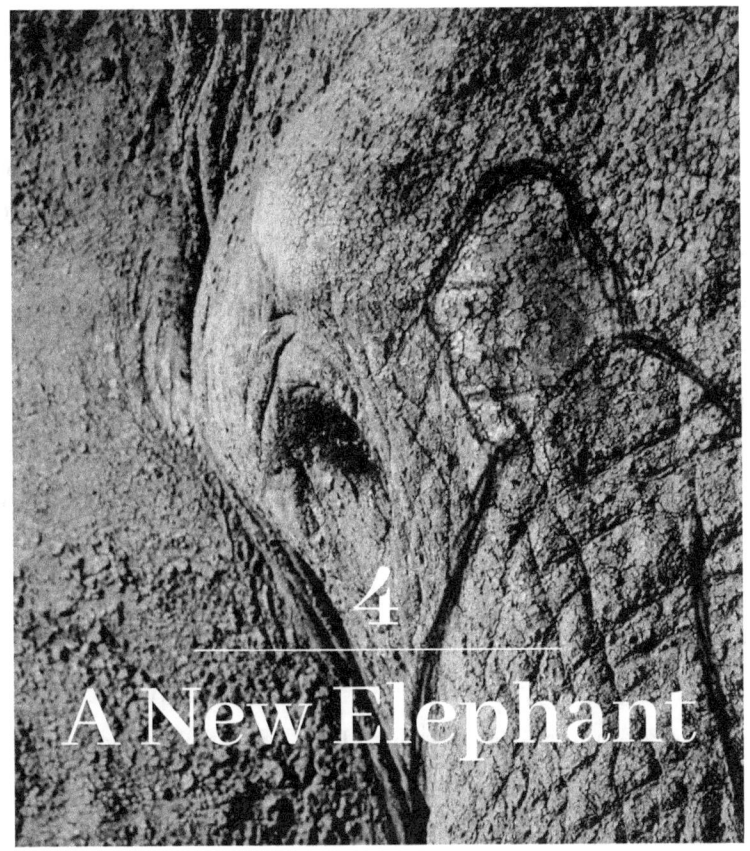

4

A New Elephant

At the beginning of the last quarter of 2001 I had a remarkable encounter with a Knysna elephant which indicated that they were beginning to know me – just as I suspected they knew Wilfred and Karel.

On a very pleasant Sunday morning I walked along the edge of the plantation where I had discovered the presence of Strangefoot and The Youngster months before. I was walking down a long straight track that ran east to west when suddenly and unexpectedly I heard the loud sound of a tree crashing to the ground about 50 metres away. This immediately tore me from my Sunday morning reverie. I froze and listened intently.

To my delight I heard an elephant feeding on the fallen tree.

Unfortunately a wall of high fynbos vegetation prevented me from actually seeing the elephant. I tried to approach from further down the track, but at the bottom of the incline dry and crackling leaves beneath my feet and a fickle wind prevented me from approaching from that direction to attempt a sighting.

I quietly returned to where I had heard the tree crashing to the ground and heard intermittent sounds of the elephant feeding. I climbed a small embankment, but I could still not see anything.

Resigned to the fact that I would not see the elephant, I marked the spot near the wall of fynbos with branches, and headed back up the track, telling myself I would return the following morning to investigate further.

Early the next morning I was walking down the east/west track when suddenly, to my surprise, I saw elephant tracks heading upwards on the track, and in places they partially covered my footprints from the day before. It was as though the elephant had been following my footprints by scent.

I continued down the track to where I had heard the tree fall and where I had heard the elephant feeding behind the wall of fynbos – the spot I had marked with branches the day before. I saw it was at that very spot that the elephant had emerged onto the track after feeding on the fallen tree – and it was there that it continued up the track following my footprints.

It was as if the elephant had been curious to seek me out.

In October 2001 I discovered a truly enchanted place – The Secret Place of the Elephants. Inadvertently, it was this discovery that would lead me in the months ahead to my very first sighting of a mysterious being – a sighting that still astounds me all these years later.

Finding The Secret Place was the result of my cautious probing explorations further and further into remote portions of the elephants' range. I deliberately use the word 'cautious' because I was working alone, and I had to learn about the different areas thoroughly so that I would never become lost.

When I got to know an area well, I would name it – such as 'Bentley's circuit' or 'Jim's central plantation route' – and then introduce Fransje to the area. By her knowing the routes, and me telling her each morning which route I would be walking that particular day, Fransje would at least know where I had gone should anything happen to me or if I was not back home at a certain time. It was just a sensible precaution.

And this was how I found The Secret Place. I was exploring further and further into the foothills of the Outeniqua Mountains. The tracks that led into the foothills were impassable for vehicles because fallen trees were strewn across them at intervals – some of which I suspected the elephants were responsible for. It was a place of no human footprints and of no human voices – a peaceful and serene place.

One bright morning as I walked in the foothills, I began coming across elephant droppings and feeding signs with increasing frequency – some quite fresh and others older, to varying degrees. I felt excited, sensing that I had inadvertently found an important part of the elephants' range, and I wondered what was drawing them so consistently to this particular area.

As I turned a corner on the trail I encountered a wet and muddy section and saw where a young elephant had lain down on the sodden soil, leaving imprints of its wrinkles and folds in the ground. It had been there less than a day before.

I continued onwards for about fifty paces and I discovered what was almost magically drawing the elephants to the area.

There on the hillside was a softly pulsating spring – a pool of water of the greatest clarity. In the centre of the small spring there was activity – specks of sand lifting and falling, dancing almost, mobilised by the pulse of the upward pushing water.

Surrounded by abundant signs of the elephants, new and old, I knew that I had found a place of almost tangible power. I drank from the spring and afterwards felt energised and reinvigorated.

Elephants are connoisseurs of water. Although the spring was small, perhaps no more than a square metre in extent, elephants were clearly coming from afar to drink from its offering, and perhaps they had been doing this for hundreds of years.

Beside the pool an elephant pathway led to the neck of a valley, and I headed down into it. Hidden at the base of the trail was a glade, shielded from view by the canopies of forest trees. On the northern side of the glade was a wall of grey rock. Without even thinking about a name for this place, the word 'Cathedral' came to mind. Like the spring, it had a sense of power. There in the centre of the glade I saw that elephants would regularly come simply to stand there.

In the first few months of the New Year, the Knysna elephants were to continue to reveal their presence to Wilfred, Karel and me.

At the end of March, Wilfred and Karel were informed that fresh elephant tracks and droppings had been found in the western area, in a place known as the Farleigh Plantations. Seldom before had it been known for the elephants to range so far west. So evidence of elephant in this area drew much attention and interest amongst foresters and forestry workers alike.

Wilfred and Karel's major role as forest guards was to monitor reports of the elephants and, when the opportunity arose, they were tasked with tracking and attempting to photograph the elephants for identification purposes. Criteria set by the forestry department management were that clear photographs with defining features (primarily tusk shape and ear notches) were required before any photographed elephants would be accepted by management as being 'new'. This was an incredibly difficult task for Wilfred and Karel to achieve in dense forest and often even denser mountain fynbos country (in some places mature fynbos vegetation is three or four metres high). But with incredible self-motivation – and at no little risk to themselves, since they were totally unarmed – these two men set out daily on their task.

As I grew to know the two men better, I could see that their determination was centred firstly in their total belief that more Knysna elephants existed than the forestry management gave credence to – and secondly they were motivated by their pure love and admiration for these amazing elephant survivors. Such love and admiration was not generally historically shared by forestry management who, for many decades, had a less than positive attitude towards the elephants.

On the report of fresh elephant signs in the Farleigh Plantations, Wilfred and Karel went to the place early in the morning and began to track a single elephant. It was going to be a long day.

The elephant was heading east. In the late afternoon they caught a glimpse of it – a quick passing view of an ear and the flash of a hindquarter.

Early the following morning they set out again on the elephant's tracks. In the late afternoon, as the elephant continued eastwards, they found the place where it had climbed down into the steep Knysna River valley, crossed the tannin brown waters and then climbed up out of the valley.

Yet again, early the next morning they continued on the trail of the elephant. Tracking elephant in the Knysna forest and in the mountain fynbos is very difficult, and cannot be compared with tracking savannah elephants anywhere else in Africa. Visibility is usually only a few metres ahead of one, and leaf litter on the ground in the forest and interwoven vegetation in the mountain fynbos rarely betray footprints. Even when the elephants walk on forest tracks, the substrate is often so hard and stony that it is difficult to see their footprints. I have demonstrated this to myself many times while on the forest tracks. One can look back where one has just stepped and often one cannot see where one had trodden a moment before.

Here the art of elephant tracking is less looking at the ground and more perceiving subtle channels of space in the vegetation, the ancient elephant pathways where grey hide brushes against trees, and by anticipating the way of the elephant. By doing this (if you got it right), you might be rewarded by finding torn branches along the pathways where the elephant had paused to feed. The biggest reward (after perhaps glimpsing a portion of the elephant's anatomy – and even then, not being entirely sure what part of the elephant it belongs to) is coming across fresh droppings.

Attempting to find elephants in the often dark, dank recesses of the forest and in the elephant maze-ways of the tall fynbos is hard and daunting work. Imagine meeting a mysterious being in such places ... In both vegetation types, the foliage crushes you, and the fragments of blue sky you can see above beckon your soul to be out in the open again and to embrace wide vistas.

Such was the daily realm of Wilfred and Karel's workplace.

Once again the following morning the two men continued on the often veiled passage of the elephant as it headed towards the Maraiskop forest, a large patch of indigenous forest singularly centred in mountain fynbos country and both surrounded and choked by a sea of pine plantations.

It was just minutes after they entered the indigenous forest that they saw a large grey shape, almost like an immense slab of granite, low on the ground.

Karel saw it first. Eyes wide, he motioned to Wilfred who, ever ready, was holding his video camera in anticipation. The 'rock' was only 20 metres away. It was a young female elephant asleep on the ground. Neither of the men had ever seen this elephant before – yet another 'new' Knysna elephant.

What occurred next happened in a flurry. The elephant's eyelashes moved and she woke up. Wilfred was already filming. The elephant heaved her great bulk upwards and stood there, looking down at the two men.

The watchers had become the watched.

Under any other circumstances, on seeing humans in such proximity, a wild elephant would, at the very least, lunge forward, and if the humans were very lucky it would then spin around and crash away through the foliage.

But this elephant did not do this. Despite the almost suicidally short distance between the men and the elephant, Wilfred continued filming. This was possibly because he was seeing the elephant through the camera viewfinder and so felt a false sense of security, a detachment from the reality of the situation. Or perhaps he felt unthreatened.

The elephant stepped forward.

Karel sensibly fled.

The elephant continued to step forward.

Wilfred crouched behind a yellowwood tree and continued to film. I have seen the footage he captured that day. It is extraordinary. It shows an almost ground to sky view of the young female elephant. She looked down at him, curved her trunk against her head, and rumbled loudly. She then stepped back to where she had been sleeping. She simply stood there for a while with only her trunk moving, pulling in the scents around her, including that of Wilfred.

Her behaviour and reaction towards the men was unusual. Elephants do not, under such circumstances, react as she did. Something else was at play here. There was familiarity. Because she knew the one filming her – and the one who fled – she had felt unthreatened.

Wilfred stayed with her and continued filming until finally, calmly, she turned and became lost to his eyes in the forest.

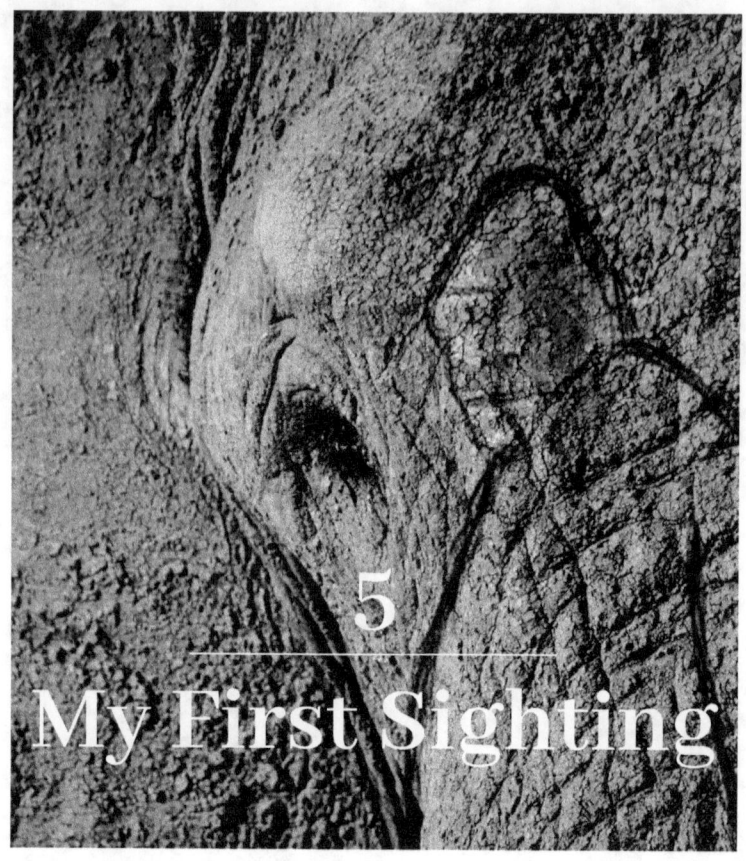

5

My First Sighting

The Guardian Newspaper 7/17/2009. Question to scientists, philosophers, artists and journalists – What will change everything? Reply by Professor Richard Dawkins: *The discovery of relict populations of extinct hominids such as* Homo erectus *and* Australopithecus *... if it happened, it would change everything.*

After discovering The Secret Place, I often visited this enchanted area. So often did I go there that a remarkable 'game' developed between the elephants and me. After leaving the spring, I placed rocks on the boughs of the trees that lay at intervals across the track – as I have mentioned, I suspected that the elephants deliberately pulled trees across the track to make it impassable for vehicles. On return visits to The Secret Place, I would repeatedly see that the elephants had removed the rocks, placing them or pushing them down onto the ground. In turn, I would stack them back up again. And so this would continue, a form of communication between the elephants and me with the rocks acting as our calling cards.

One morning in May I visited The Secret Place. As I walked around the last corner before the spring, I saw a pile of very fresh droppings. I was about to investigate these and the equally fresh elephant footprints when I heard movement down below in the Cathedral valley. Elephants! After peering down into the valley, but not seeing anything, I walked on very quietly to the spring. There I saw many fresh feeding signs – young Cape beech trees torn down and blackwood leaves covering the ground like sprinkled green confetti.

Near the spring, next to recently torn bunches of sedges, were the clear footprints of Strangefoot – and further along the path were the smaller ones of The Youngster.

Suddenly, down in the Cathedral, I heard the sharp snapping of a branch. The elephants were less than seventy paces from where I was standing. By throwing some dust into the air, I tested the direction of the breeze. It was in my favour. The breeze was drifting softly from the direction of the elephants to me.

As I was trying to find a vantage point from which I could look down to catch a glimpse of the elephants, a loud trumpeting erupted below me in the valley. The piercing sound echoed repeatedly all around me, reverberating off the slopes of the valley, drumming into my ears and head. My heart began to pound and I quickly tested the wind again. It was still in my favour.

Calming down somewhat, I realised that the trumpeting had been caused by some interaction between the two elephants – it had nothing to do with my presence. Feeding sounds continued. All was peaceful.

From another vantage point, I saw movement as the elephants' bodies brushed against the vegetation. Getting a full sighting no longer mattered to me. I knew where they were and who they were and that was priceless. I felt immensely privileged to be at the beautiful Secret Place, many kilometres from the nearest person and less than seventy paces away from two of the most special elephants on earth.

Then, some weeks later, I saw it – a mysterious being. It was a clear sunny Sunday and I had trekked to The Secret Place early in the morning and as usual found signs of the elephants there. When I left I replaced the rocks they had removed from the boughs of the trees and headed towards where I had left my vehicle.

An hour or so later I was walking westwards on an infrequently used track. To my left was a stand of pine trees. The sky that mid-morning was the brightest blue, the air was invigorating, and I was feeling clear-headed. I was looking forward to taking Fransje to lunch, as we did most Sundays, at an outdoor restaurant that overlooked a stunning beach on the Indian Ocean.

It was a perfect day and the very last thing on my mind was mysterious hominoids.

Suddenly I felt that I was being watched and I instantly became alert.

In the many years that I have roamed the wilds of Africa, I have always been aware of when another might be watching me – be it a person or an animal. I can sense somehow when hidden eyes are observing me.

In the case of a hidden predator, I learnt many years ago not to stop and look around for it, as this might provoke an aggressive response, but to continue walking, and to scan around casually. Stopping can be interpreted by a predator as a threat.

Therefore, that bright Sunday morning I reacted as I always did when I sensed I was being watched. I walked on, casually looking to my left, towards the pine plantation.

There, partially hidden behind a pine tree while peering at me, I saw it: a hominoid being covered in russet hair. It was approximately forty paces away. Shocked, but pretending I had not seen it, I carried on walking, watching it as long as I could from the corner of my eye.

1st Sighting
2002#. Peering from behind tree at me *
Approx 5 foot high.

I continued walking for approximately a kilometre and a half before I turned to look behind me. Seeing nothing, I sank heavily to the ground. I was utterly bewildered by what I had seen. As I sat there on the ground I felt as though I was enveloped in a numbing fog, a cloud of grey on that bright blue-sky day. I held my head in my hands, my fingers covering my eyes.

My initial reaction to seeing the strange being had been controlled, honed by years of avoidance of potentially provoking an aggressive response from a predator. I had walked on. My second response, numbness and confusion, was a new reaction.

I do not know how long I sat there on the ground, but gradually the grey fog lifted enough for me to stand up and to walk on. I was approximately four kilometres from where I had left the vehicle. As I walked, my head began to clear somewhat and I tried to analyse what I had seen.

Despite the shocking image I had seen peering at me from behind the tree, I sensed the curiosity of the being and, something which is almost impossible to explain, I sensed that it was female. I sensed that, combined with its curiosity, it had also been benign in its nature. It had not been overly fearful, though in retrospect, I thought that if I had not carried on walking, but had turned to face it, it would have moved out of sight.

It was then that I wondered: how many times had it seen me before, over the months that I had been repeatedly trekking to and from The Secret Place? Was I a familiar stranger to the being?

As I walked, I began to think about what she looked like (from this point onwards I will refer to the being as a 'she'). She was clearly upright standing and appeared to be covered in hair that was russet in colour. I had not seen her face clearly. That part of her head seemed to be partially covered in shadow. I estimated that she would have been approximately five feet and three inches in height. She had been leaning slightly to her right from behind the tree, and during the glimpses I had of her, she appeared not to move, but to be looking in my direction with what seemed to be curiosity.

I eventually reached the car and in somewhat of a daze I drove from the high country, through the forest down the deep Gouna River gorge, and up on to the ridge where we lived overlooking the Knysna lagoon and the Indian Ocean.

There, at the house, I told Fransje what I had seen and experienced. For some strange reason (perhaps because of the shocked state I was in at the time) I do not remember her reaction. I contacted Fransje recently to ask her of her memories of that day.

Fransje told me, 'I remember that day clearly. You were pretty shocked, Gareth. Though you also appeared to be confused, you were adamant that what you had seen was not a person peering at you from behind the tree, and yet you were also adamant it was not an animal. You were also adamant it was standing upright and that it would walk on two legs like a person. Juan's story,' she continued, 'about the German tourists and what they had seen was clearly on your mind. We spoke about how it was very likely that what you had seen that Sunday was what the tourists had seen. The experience preoccupied you intensely for some time afterwards. Though initially it baffled you, you spoke about the experience a lot. The day came, though, when you simply accepted that you had seen what you had seen, and that it was a type of hominoid.'

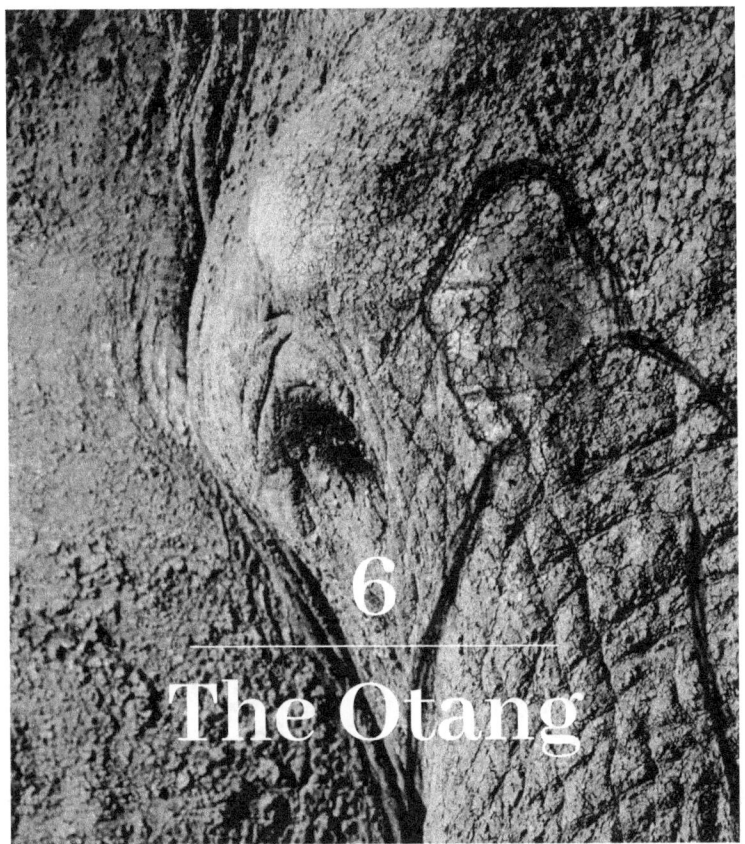

6
The Otang

'Mysterious', 'magical' and 'mystical'. These terms are often used in books and articles when describing the Knysna forest. As I mentioned at the beginning of this book, I knew very little about the dense Afromontane forest – and today, eighteen years later, I still see this place as a great unknown. And this keeps one humble here.

I had come from a background of two decades of working for the greater protection of lions – and elephants – in dry and relatively open bush country in which one can learn the ways of the land fairly quickly. Not so the forest. The forest ecosystem and the surrounding mountain fynbos could not have been a greater contrast to the land of wide vistas, and a constant horizon, that I had known for so long.

Over the years journalists have commented that by coming to the Knysna forest and studying the elephants, I had 'switched species'. This not accurate, though. As I have said, wherever I had worked for lions, I had always acted to protect elephants. The reality of the situation was that one of the few commonalities between my home in dry bush lands and in the forest and mountain fynbos was elephants!

When I began the elephant study, I was familiar with virtually none of the some 400 species of forest plants and trees. The Knysna forest covers over 600 square kilometres. South Africa is predominantly a dry country, and forests represent only 0.5 per cent of the country's landmass. In the savannah lands I had previously lived in, the average annual rainfall was a mere 310 millimetres, and restricted to summer months only. In contrast, these forests receive in excess of some 750 millimetres annually, with rain falling throughout the year.

The mountain fynbos areas beyond the forests, where the elephants frequently roam – in fact, as I quickly learnt, this is the main habitat of the elephants – was also staggeringly new to me. The Cape fynbos makes up four-fifths of the Cape Floral Kingdom (one of the world's six floral kingdoms), comprising more than 8 600 plant species, of which 5 800 are endemic and exist nowhere else on earth.

Therefore, apart from the bird species, the only other aspect of the area I was really familiar with was elephants! And of course the host of other mammal species such as leopard, bushbuck, bushpig, honey badger and others whose adaptability allows them to range in both forest and bush country.

On reflection today, the whole situation I had found myself in was a paradox. I, the outsider to the place, knew virtually nothing about the habitat and the workings of the ecosystems – but I knew about elephants.

In contrast, the forestry managers and government scientists knew the ecosystems extremely well but, as I was to discover, did not know too much about elephants or elephant behaviour. Perhaps the only thing we had in common was an (unspoken) incomprehension of a mysterious hominoid that was said to exist there.

Others, though, hold knowledge of the mysterious beings. There exists a small population of local people who have lived in the vicinity of the forests and the mountain fynbos for their entire lives. They know about these beings, and view them as not particularly mysterious, but as part of the overall tapestry of life in the forest and fynbos.

One of these people was a remarkable old lady who became a good friend of mine; her name was Mrs Jordaan.

With her tiny, wizened features and ochre complexion, Mrs Jordaan lived in a little red-roofed house, built a hundred years before, in the southern portion of the Knysna forest alongside the main dirt road heading to the Diepwalle Forest Station. Next to her quaint house were other dwellings where her daughters and grandchildren lived.

It was from Mrs Jordaan that I learnt that the mysterious beings had a local name – the 'Otang'.

Mrs Jordaan died in 2012, at the age of eighty-two. She was probably the very last of her generation of the original first people of the southern Cape – the San people. Her parents and uncles and aunts had worked as virtual slaves on one of the sprawling sheep farms owned by descendants of the original white settlers in the semi-desert land of the Karoo to the north of the forest and the Outeniqua Mountains range.

To put into perspective the perplexing times in which Mrs Jordaan had lived, in the year of her birth (1930) white women were given the right to vote in South Africa. Yet it was only in 1936, that the last permit to hunt a San woman (in neighbouring South-West Africa, now Namibia) had been issued. Mrs Jordaan would have been in her mid-sixties when she herself voted for the very first time in 1994.

$$\sim\!\!\bigcirc$$

Mrs Jordaan married a Xhosa forestry worker and moved from the Karoo. The Knysna forest was to be her home for the rest of her life. My move from open savannah to the forests more than sixty years later in a sense mirrored the contrast of Mrs Jordaan's move from the big sky and the dry land of the Karoo to the great forests.

Residing at the Diepwalle Forest Station, and later at the Gouna Forest Station, she had four children, one being a son called Booi, who was the catalyst for my meeting Mrs Jordaan for the very first time – and it was from her that I learnt more about the mysterious beings that she and her family referred to as the 'otang'.

I first met Booi one Sunday morning on the main forest road as I was driving towards the Diepwalle Forest Station. For many months I had driven past the little settlement where Mrs Jordaan and her family lived, but apart from mutual waves and smiles as I passed by, I had not met the people. That was to change that Sunday morning.

Booi, a man in his forties, was walking on the forest road heading from Knysna to visit his mother, sisters, nieces and nephews. This I learnt was a Sunday routine of his. Hearing my vehicle, he flagged me down, indicating that he would like a lift. He was still slightly the worse for wear from the night before (his own admission), but spoke eloquently and with fondness about the forest and its denizens and of his family who had lived alongside the forest road for so many years.

'You must meet my mother and the family,' Booi said, as we approached the little settlement.

'I would love to, thank you, Booi,' I replied.

We parked under a tree on the edge of the road, and then walked up a little pathway that led to his mother's delightful little red-roofed house. Booi's nieces and nephews scampered up to us saying their hellos with happy faces. As we approached the house, cradled by rose bushes, plum trees and banana palms, a tiny figure emerged from the front door – Mrs Jordaan.

In the months ahead I would regularly stop off at Mrs Jordaan's to visit her and the family. One of Mrs Jordaan's daughters (or Booi, if it was a Sunday) would act as interpreter. Mrs Jordaan spoke little English and I spoke even less of the heavily accented and unique southern Cape Afrikaans which is the lingua franca of the Knysna forest people.

Initially it was the secretive elephants that we would speak about, with me telling her about my research, and she telling me of the times she had encountered the elephants over the long years she had lived there.

Mrs Jordaan often spoke about an old female elephant who she called the *ou dame* (the old lady), known by the white foresters as 'The Matriarch'. It was this elephant that the foresters and forestry scientists mistakenly thought, back in 1999, was the very last remaining Knysna elephant. Wise Mrs Jordaan knew differently. Translated into English, she would say 'The forests are big, much bigger than to hide just a single elephant. There are of course the *ou dame se kinders* (the old lady's children) and the *kinders se kinders*. And we must not forget the big men either.'

'Yes,' she would continue, 'the *ou dame* walked frequently on our road here (pointing at the Diepwalle Forest Station road just beyond her house). She would come to check on us. She knew us.'

Chuckling about the retelling of tales of the *ou dame*, Mrs Jordaan often said with a questioning face, '*Ou dame?* I first came to this forest before the *ou dame* was even born! So who is the real *ou dame* here?'

When I asked her about the other Knysna elephants, she would always say, 'Why do you ask me of this, Gareth? You know of others – so why do you ask me of this? That is your job!'

One day, and I cannot remember how it happened, our conversation turned to what she referred to as the otang. And that day Mrs Jordaan told me a most remarkable story.

Many years ago when her children were small and the family was living at the Gouna Forest Station, an extraordinary encounter took place. It was an encounter that was to remain etched clearly in Mrs Jordaan's mind for the rest of her life. Mrs Jordaan had had a full and protracted sighting of an otang.

Long before the sighting, she and her husband (and other forest people) would from time to time come across otang footprints, some large, others small. Mrs Jordaan and the other forest people were respectful of the otangs, but not necessarily fearful of them. After all no one could remember the otangs doing any harm to anyone.

To Mrs Jordaan and the other forest people it seemed that the otangs were active primarily, but not exclusively, at night. Occasionally, late in the night, to the utter consternation of the occupants of vehicles, they would be seen dashing across lonely forest roads, lit dramatically by the car's headlights. Also, when fresh footprints were found this would usually be early in the mornings, tracks made the night before.

'They are like the elephants, Gareth,' Mrs Jordaan would say. 'They like the solitude and secretiveness, but,' she would sometimes add, 'a few of them are curious about us forest people. Like the one that I watched for about fifteen minutes one night.'

The first time Mrs Jordaan told me this, my jaw dropped.

The incident occurred one night at her home at the Gouna Forest Station when her husband was away, and when her children were tucked up in bed and sound asleep. Mrs Jordaan was sitting knitting at her kitchen table, her face glowing in the light of the paraffin lamp. All was quiet and calm. That was until she heard faint movements outside her kitchen door – and when her dog Tammy, who was lying at her feet, began uttering low growls.

For a moment she was convinced that the handle of the kitchen door moved. She wondered who could possibly be walking around so late at night.

Mrs Jordaan put her knitting down on the table, rose quietly and stepped across to a cabinet where she kept her torch. She switched it on, walked to the kitchen sink, above which was the open kitchen window, and shone the torch through it.

She could not see anything apart from the ghostly shadow of the old red alder tree, approximately 15 metres away next to her little vegetable patch. Shaking her head slightly, she turned off the torch and returned to the kitchen table, and to her knitting.

A little later as she was about to get ready to go to bed, Tammy began to growl again and Mrs Jordaan saw that the hair on her back was raised.

Again she reached for her torch, went to the sink and shone the light through the window. It was then that she saw an extraordinary sight. Standing next to her vegetable patch, where she grew sweet potatoes, spinach and tomatoes, was a broad-shouldered and muscular man-like figure. It was covered in dark hair.

'Otang!' she gasped quietly.

Trembling slightly, she watched as the otang shifted its upper torso to the left and the right, as if to avoid the light and to see what was behind the beam. This continued for many minutes until suddenly the otang turned its head towards the nearby road, as if listening, and in the blink of an eye, moved away and was gone. Mrs Jordaan gasped again. She had never before seen anything move with such swiftness, not even the swallows that nested below the eaves of the roof in the summertime. The otang had simply vanished.

She shone the torch around for a little while, but saw nothing. She closed the window, returned to the table, sat down, and now in a somewhat shocked state, thought about what she had seen. Some minutes later she was pulled from her thoughts when she heard a truck approaching in the distance on the road beyond her vegetable patch. She listened as it rumbled closer and closer. It passed her home and its rumbles then became fainter and fainter.

Mrs Jordaan realised that it was the truck that the otang had heard from afar. At the time, she had not heard anything.

After about ten minutes she surprised herself by deciding to unlock and open the kitchen door and to shine her torch around the outside. As she stepped slightly outside, shining all around, she immediately smelt a pungent odour in the still night air. It reminded her of the smell of a worked, sweating horse. It was the otang's smell. She stepped back inside and locked the door. Mrs Jordaan did not sleep much that night.

Early the next morning, as the sun was rising through a stretch of forest in the east, Mrs Jordaan ventured outside and walked up to her little vegetable patch. There on the ground beside some of her tomato plants were clear footprints. When she saw these she knew that she had not imagined nor dreamt the events of the night before.

Hearing the faint voices of her waking children, she turned and, in a daze, returned to the little house.

Over the years Mrs Jordaan often retold this story to me, and the details of the sequence of events never changed. I always assumed that the otang she had seen was of medium height, like the one I had seen. On one of the last occasions she told me the story, I interjected and asked, 'And it was about this height?' indicating the top of my chest.

Mrs Jordaan looked at me with mock annoyance, and spoke rapidly. The translation given by her daughter was, 'No, Gareth. Why do you not listen carefully? It was not that height! I told you before, it was at least (indicating with her hands the measurement of approximately a foot) this much taller than you!'

I was amazed. This meant that the otang Mrs Jordaan had observed that extraordinary night had been over seven feet tall.[3]

---

3 Soon after Mrs Jordaan first told me about her encounter with the otang, I photocopied a page of drawings from a book on hominoids and one day I showed it to her. Mrs Jordaan grew excited when she saw the illustrations, saying, 'Yes, the otang I saw was like these ones!' I gave her the copy of the drawings. One day, years later, when visiting her with Booi, and discussing the otang, she went into her little home and emerged with the neatly folded copy of the drawings (see the photo section).

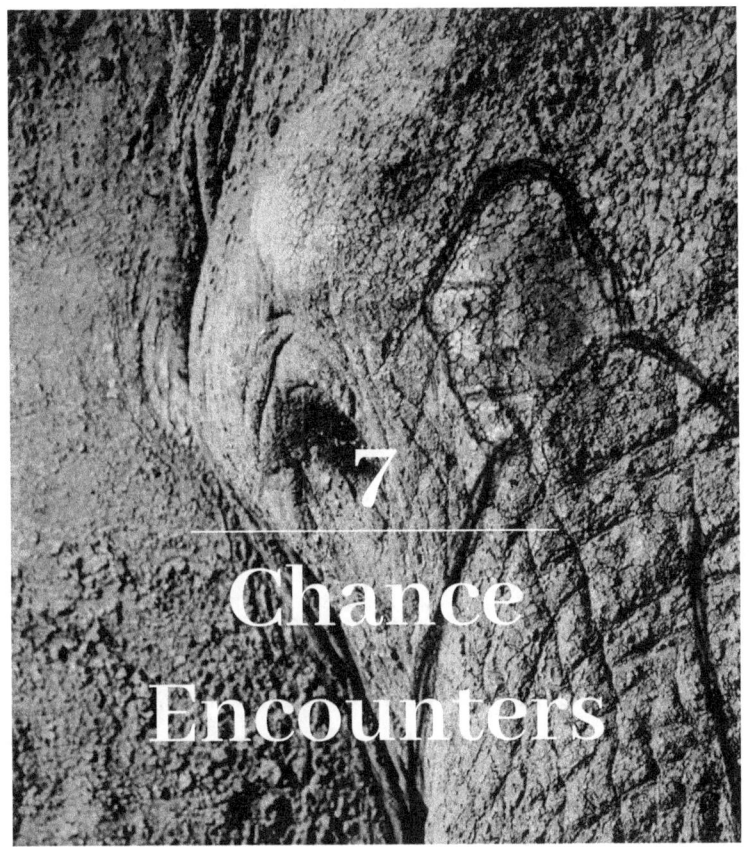

7

Chance
Encounters

O tang exists. Of this there was no doubt. It had all begun in 1999 when Fransje and I were told about the German tourists' encounter. This was followed by the forestry scientist telling me about two separate otang sightings reported by forestry workers, and my neighbour's colleague telling me of his and his brother's childhood sighting. All this culminated in my own unexpected sighting which left me shocked and confused. And then, of course, there was Mrs Jordaan recounting her protracted sighting of the tall otang. Yes, otang exists, but how was I to proceed with this astonishing discovery?

I decided that, without attracting attention, I would undertake my own research in the field, investigate other local reported sightings of otang, and research what had been written and recorded about possible relict hominoids in other parts of Africa and elsewhere in the world. (As you will read in a later chapter, this would lead me to make contact with a wildlife researcher and a nature photographer in Sumatra who had repeated sightings of similar beings.) My otang research and investigation was to become a parallel study to my ongoing research on the Knysna elephants.

One day during this time I was at the Diepwalle Forest Station being assisted with elephant food plant identification by two forestry employees who worked in the forest station's indigenous nursery. One man was an older gentleman who had worked in the department for his entire life. The other man was much younger and was college educated.

Both men knew me fairly well, knew of my work on the elephants and, as just mentioned, would from time to time (patiently) assist me with the identification of elephant food plants. Their knowledge of the forest trees and plants was immense, and in this regard they were very much my teachers and I learnt much from them. For this I am greatly indebted to them.

That particular morning neither of the men knew that I would be bringing up the subject of the otang, something we had never before spoken about. Therefore their answers and comments were completely spontaneous which gave great credibility to what they had to say.

I began the discussion by telling the men about the German tourists' encounter with three otangs on the Diepwalle road back in 1999. After relating this incident the younger man turned to me immediately and told me that his father (who had also worked for the forestry department) had had a sighting of an otang, and that it had been at night. His father was driving to Diepwalle from Knysna and near an area known as Veldmanspad (a kilometre or so from where Mrs Jordaan and her family lived), a bipedal being suddenly ran at speed across the road. He saw it clearly in the vehicle's headlights. The younger man then said to me, 'Gareth, these beings seem to be very much like us, that is, human-like.'

I thought this was an interesting comment and observation, and it mirrored my own feelings about the otang. From the experience of my own sighting, I distinctly felt that the being was human-like, as opposed to being a member of the great apes. I had felt a sense of relatedness to it.

As I was thinking about this, the older man began telling me that eighteen months before his brother-in-law had also seen, again at night and from a vehicle, an otang dash across the road. He went on to mention that just eight months ago a group of forestry workers in a commercial plantation collectively claimed to have seen an otang.

My forestry colleagues' information that morning was fascinating. Within a relatively short conversation I had learnt of two compelling sightings, both at night and both from vehicles, by the two men's direct family members. This indicated, or at least suggested, that otang sightings were perhaps not uncommon. Both men's accounts were very frank and matter of fact, indicating that they very much viewed the existence of the otang as a flesh and blood being ('human-like' as the younger man had said), and not belonging to the realm of spirit or superstition.

I long ago learnt that one should not actively search for otangs or the Knysna elephants. To do so seems to go against natural law here. These beings will simply appear at an appropriate time. I have no idea what governs or determines this, but to seek them out is to be ultimately counterproductive to a lesser or greater degree.

Understanding this was one of the reasons why I decided to stop visiting The Secret Place of the Elephants.

It is the most beautiful, magical and peaceful place in the entire forest and mountain fynbos range of the elephants. I had been so privileged to learn much about the secret elephants there. It was where, with the rocks on the boughs of the strewn trees, I had communicated with the elephants. And it was when returning from The Secret Place that I had my very first sighting of an otang.

But I decided one day not to go back there again.

It was not that I no longer wanted to return but, firstly, I felt my regular visits might ultimately attract, or draw, those who wished to see the elephants not necessarily for the right reasons. On each visit, a kind of guilt filled me and I felt as though betrayal was lurking close to me, like a shadow following me.

Also, with each visit, until the very last one, I felt increasingly as though I was pushing the boundaries of my endeavours. I knew that as long as I continued going to The Secret Place, the greater the chances were of experiencing increased magical encounters with the elephants – and perhaps even with the otang that had spied on me those long months before – but intuitively I knew that something could also change, or even snap.

To keep visiting, I realised, I risked bringing betrayal to the elephants, and to the very place itself, to its peace and its magic. And so I never returned – but my memories of the place are etched deeply in my mind and will never leave me.

I had listened with my heart and it was the right decision.

By not actually looking for the mysterious elephants, or the even more mysterious otangs, they simply appear! How many times I have experienced this phenomenon.

Once, accompanied by my German shepherd Akera, I set out on a Sunday morning to do some leopard research some six kilometres north of where we lived. I planned to measure tracks, and upon finding scat, collect a portion for diet analysis. Suddenly and quite unexpectedly, from no more than 50 metres away, I had my first full view of a Knysna elephant. It was a youngster of about six or seven years old. I had just moments before missed seeing its mother crossing the track ahead of me, but as I watched the youngster (and as it watched me) I could hear her moving nearby in the dense vegetation.

Akera and I backed away and headed home. I was overjoyed, yet at the same time shocked by the sighting.

My first sighting of an otang was yet another example of how these beings just appear when the time is right. That morning, as I have said, the very last thing on my mind was a bipedal hominoid.

Here is another example. Months after I had seen the large calf, while walking our dogs one late afternoon in some high country that overlooked harvested plantations interspersed with stands of pines, Fransje and I spied from afar the (presumably) same mother and calf.

Incredibly, through binoculars, we watched them for almost an hour – and we had simply gone out that afternoon to walk the dogs!

On yet another occasion, when I was walking to The Secret Place I saw, in a flash, a leopard leaping away from a distance of just three metres. I do not think it was coincidence that later that day was one of the very few occasions I found no fresh signs of the elephants at The Secret Place. It had been my day to encounter a leopard instead.

And then there was the incident during the filming of our documentary on the elephants (somewhat ironically entitled *The Search for the Knysna Elephants* and which was later screened internationally) when, a full two weeks after my film-maker friend Mark van Wijk and his film crew's fruitless search for the elephants, in the very last hour of the very last day of filming an elephant simply showed itself. The film crew had only minutes before resigned themselves to the fact that they would never film a Knysna elephant.

So, one must not seek out these beings. It goes against natural law here, and it is at best inappropriate to actively search for them.

They appear magically, simply on their own terms.

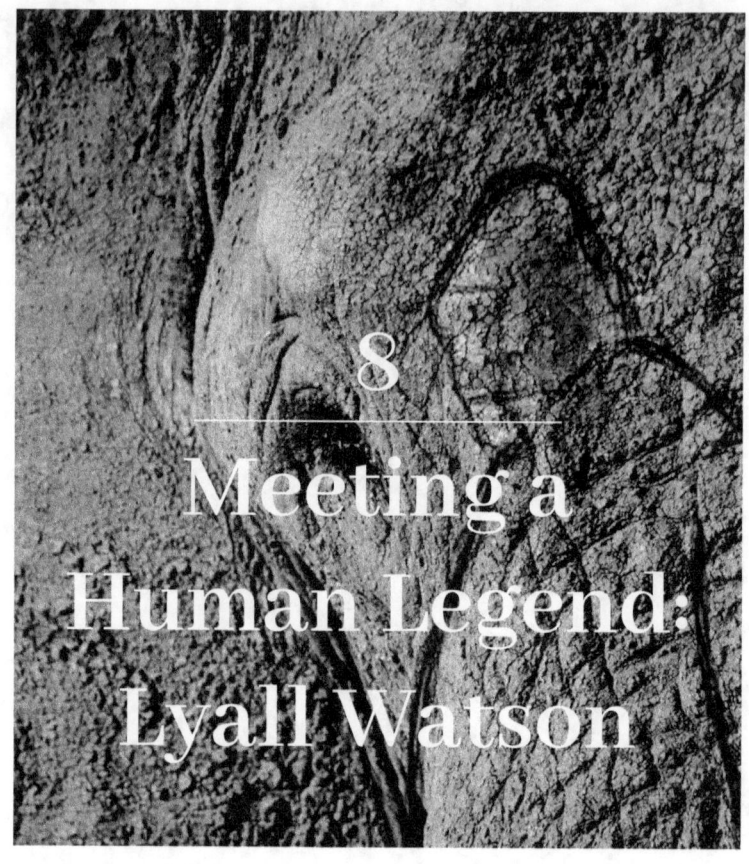

8

Meeting a Human Legend: Lyall Watson

'If we do one day come across another form of life, a sentient being, which I hope we do, because it would be marvellous and very exciting, but it might be so different, that unless you are prepared to accept vast differences, you might not experience it at all.'

— So said the late great Lyall Watson

In this statement Lyall could have been referring to the otangs.

Lyall was an exceptional man and he was a friend of mine. He was also a lifelong friend of the Knysna elephants. He was a botanist, biologist, ecologist, ethologist, anthropologist and the author of twenty-four books, most of which dealt with an array of subjects that he described as 'the soft edges of science'. Of this he once said:

It is here, it seems, that we get fleeting glimpses of strange shadows just beneath the surface of current understanding. Such will-o-the wisps, I suspect, may be our best chance of some sort of reconciliation between hard science and softer, more organic, human experience.

His was a brilliant mind. Lyall entered university at just fifteen years of age. By the time he was nineteen he had completed degrees in zoology and botany. He went on to gain degrees involving geology, marine biology, ecology and chemistry. Lyall earned his doctorate at the University of London working under Desmond Morris, the acclaimed author of *The Naked Ape*.

Supernature, published in 1973, was Lyall's most famous and most popular book. It dealt with inexplicable and mysterious phenomena. He told me how the book had been rejected multiple times and it was only two years after he had written it that it was finally published. The book became a sensation. It topped the best-seller list for some fifty weeks. It went into ten reprints in ten weeks and sold over three quarters of a million copies in paperback. How the publishers who rejected the book must have cringed.

Lyall died in 2008, aged sixty-nine, of complications of Lewy body dementia – a little understood disease that combines the symptoms of Alzheimer's and Parkinson's disease. The second last book Lyall wrote was the superbly titled *Elephantoms*; part memoir, it deals with Lyall's lifelong fascination for elephants in general and the Knysna elephants in particular. And this book was the catalyst for Lyall's and my friendship. This alone is a curious story. First, though, I must digress a little.

Elephantoms was first published in 2002 by W.W. Norton & Company. At around that time I had sent a synopsis of a book to Penguin Books (South Africa) which I had planned about the Knysna elephants. This book was to become *The Secret Elephants*. Penguin Books had previously published two of my books, and I was fairly confident that they might be interested in the elephant book. Penguin politely declined the book – and I was left a little mystified.

Little did I know that Penguin had just bought the South African paperback rights to *Elephantoms* and were to publish it the following year in 2003.

As fate was to have it, though, Penguin Books went on to publish *The Secret Elephants* in 2009.

I must add a small aside here. My editor for *The Secret Elephants* was Pam Thornley. Pam, a wonderful editor and a gracious lady, had also been the editor of the two previous books I had published with Penguin (and was to be the editor of my autobiography, *My Lion's Heart*, in 2014, published by Tracey McDonald Publishers, also the publishers of the South African edition of this book). And this is where synchronicity steps in. Back in 1965, after recently earning his PhD under Desmond Morris, Lyall had supervised Pam's Honours dissertation at Wits University. When they met again in 2003 (thirty-eight years later) when Penguin was publishing *Elephantoms*, Lyall immediately remembered Pam and the research she had done under his guidance.

As I have said, how Lyall and I met is a curious story. Ritually on Sunday evenings at our home on the edge of the Knysna forest, I would listen to a radio programme called *Believe it or Not* which at the time was South Africa's longest running radio talk show. The programme's themes included spirituality and the supernatural. The show's host is a dear friend of mine, Kate Turkington, who I have known for almost my entire adult life.

One Sunday evening in 2003, I was delighted to hear that Kate was to interview Lyall. I had long been a fan of Lyall's books, one of my favourites being *Jacobson's Organ* which explores the roles of smells and pheromones in humans, other animals, and plants.

The Knysna elephants are a major thread in the narrative of *Elephantoms* – beginning with Lyall's first encounter with a Knysna elephant as a child, and ending with him celebrating the news of my colleague Wilfred Oraai's discovery of a young adult bull elephant that no one had known existed. But I did not know this as I began to listen to the interview. I had yet to read *Elephantoms* and had no idea that the book centred on the Knysna elephants.

Towards the end of the interview Kate asked Lyall, 'Do you know my friend Gareth Patterson? He is studying the Knysna elephants at the moment.' To which Lyall replied, 'I know of Gareth's work with lions, but I had no idea he was now doing work on the elephants. Fascinating. I will be in Knysna in a few days' time promoting *Elephantoms* and I will see if my publicist at Penguin can arrange for the two of us to meet up.'

I swallowed hard when I heard this. So the book centred on the Knysna elephants. Lyall was a legendary figure to me. And it seemed that we were to meet. I knew that first thing the following morning I would have to get my hands on a copy of *Elephantoms* and read it quickly before Lyall arrived in Knysna!

I speed-read *Elephantoms*. Towards the end of the book Lyall told of an incredible encounter he had in 2000 with 'The Matriarch', the elderly Knysna female elephant that the forestry department had stated (erroneously, thank goodness) was the last living Knysna elephant. How on earth could they have been certain that she was the last elephant? It simply had not made sense. But that had become their reality in 1999. Reality is based on personal subjectivity and, as Lyall once said, if it is true that reality is partly, at least, a construct of consciousness, in other words, reality is something made by the mind, you can change it (reality), by changing your mind.

The name 'The Matriarch' did not make sense either. If the elderly female was the very last elephant, for the forestry department to have named her The Matriarch was ill conceived and un-thought out. Of this Lyall wrote in *Elephantoms*:

> The very word 'matriarch' is a compound of obligations, of an identity defined by reference to the other elephants which form her family and clan. It is a word that has no logical or biological singular. A matriarch on her own is just an elephant, and an elephant on her own is nothing.

When we met, Lyall referred to a forestry department scientist who was the main protagonist of the 'last elephant' hypothesis, as 'Dr Death', adding, 'Who would want to promote of the elephants, such a morbid and negative outlook?'

Hearing reports in the millennial year that the forestry department had maintained that the elderly female was the very last elephant brought Lyall hurriedly back to Knysna – as he relates in *Elephantoms*. One day he walked on the cliffs above the coastline where, as a child, he had seen his very first Knysna elephant.

That day upon the cliffs, at some fateful point, Lyall sat down on a rock, closed his eyes, and listened to the white noise of the sea.

When he opened his eyes, he saw a whale.

This was not a southern right whale, the whales that come close to these shores to calve in the winter months. It was summertime and the whale Lyall saw was a very rare visitor, the largest animal on planet Earth – a blue whale. Lyall was also a whale expert. In the mid-1970s he was appointed the first Seychelles Commissioner for Whales and represented the country at the International Whaling Commission where the Seychelles Resolution for an Indian Ocean whale sanctuary was successfully passed.

That day upon the cliff Lyall gauged that the whale was a female and wondered what had brought her so close to the shore. As he thought about this he heard and felt a heavy throbbing in the air. He stood up and tried to discover the source of the sound. He turned and gazed down into a nearby gorge that led down to the sea. And there he saw her – the elderly female elephant, identifiable by her broken off left tusk.

Elephants communicate with deep and powerful infrasound – sound waves with frequencies below the limit of human hearing and described by elephant, whale and bioacoustics expert Katy Payne as being like 'silent thunder'. Blue whales, too, communicate through infrasound. It was to Lyall as though the two females were talking to each other. He turned to look back to the whale and saw that she was surfacing.

He wrote of this in *Elephantoms*:

The Matriarch was here for the whale! The largest animal in the ocean and the largest living land animal were no more than a hundred yards apart, and I was convinced they were communicating. In infrasound, in concert, sharing big brains and long lives, understanding the pain of high investment in a few precious offspring, aware of the importance and pleasure of complex sociability, these rare and lovely great ladies were commiserating over the back fence of this rocky Cape shore, woman to woman, matriarch to matriarch, almost the last of their kind.

I turned, blinking away the tears, and left them to it. This was no place for a mere man ...

When I read this tears had glistened in my eyes too. Later when I thought about what Lyall had written about the elephant and the whale, I became more pragmatic. I put my researcher's hat back on.

Had Lyall really seen what he described? It had been said that elephants had been absent from that sea-facing southern portion of their range since the early 1970s, shunning the coast after the illegal killing of Adam (Aftand), the famous Knysna bull, by a forestry official.

For three decades, so I had been told by forestry officials, no tracks or droppings or feeding signs of the elephants had been found there by patrolling forest guards. I was also told that no signs of elephants had ever been reported in that area by the thousands of visitors to the place over those long years. If this was to be believed, it did suggest that, with the killing of Aftand, a grim residue of death had persisted and the coastal area had become an elephant vacuum.

Because of this assumption, I had decided not to include the coastal region in my study area when I began my research. On reflection today, that was probably a mistake. I had based the decision on the thinking that, yes, elephants are grey ghosts and can keep themselves hidden, but their droppings and tracks always betray their presence. If at some point the elephants had again begun to roam the land facing the sea, then surely someone would have found signs of them?

Wilfred and Karel had once told me that the very last time they had seen the elderly female was in the year 2000, the same year another forest guard, my friend Cyril Sam, had seen her heading southwards at midnight on the Diepwalle road. And afterwards she was never seen again, until the encounter described by Lyall in the summer of that same year.

After I finished reading *Elephantoms* I was perplexed and uncertain whether or not Lyall had witnessed the elephant and the whale in concert with each other. That was until I spent some time with the man.

Lyall was waiting for me, sitting peacefully on a wooden bench outside the lovely old stone built Knysna library. He had just spoken at a book promotion lunch. The library was an appropriate place for us to meet. I remember his kind eyes and his gentle manner.

Later in the afternoon I drove Lyall up the twisting Gouna gorge and into the central forest. We had barely entered the forest when quite unexpectedly and completely unprompted, Lyall began to tell me about the meeting of the elderly female elephant and the whale (at this point he did not know that I had read *Elephantoms*). He described the extraordinary encounter in the same way he had written about it. There was, however, one difference. Reading about the encounter, it had seemed otherworldly. Hearing Lyall telling of the encounter, it became real and unquestionable.

We walked on the forest edge for a while that late afternoon and as the sun lowered we drove back to where Fransje and I lived. There, with Fransje and Lyall's publicist, we sipped wine, chatted, and nibbled at the snacks Fransje had prepared, enjoying the peacefulness of the early evening.

At some point Lyall's publicist suggested they head back to their hotel in town. The next day was to be a busy one. They were to travel to Cape Town and continue with the busy schedule of interviews and book promotions.

Just before they left, Lyall gave me and Fransje a copy of *Elephantoms*. Inside he had inscribed:

To Gareth and Fransje:
With envy and admiration
Lyall Watson

From then onwards Lyall and I remained in regular contact. One day in an email he asked me what my physical address was as he wanted to courier a box of books to Fransje and me. Lyall had an apartment in Camps Bay in Cape Town, but was about to move to the United States.

When the box arrived we were astonished to see that it contained, amongst other things, several rare and valuable plant books, including the massive 1457-page tome, *Medicinal and Poisonous Plants of Southern and Eastern Africa* – a veritable bible for botanists. Also in the box was a beautiful stone hand axe. In a note Lyall had placed in the box, he wrote that he estimated that the stone axe was some 1.2 million years old. 'From his hand to mine across the ages and now to yours,' Lyall had written in the note.

At the bottom of the box was Lyall's personal ordinance survey map that covered the entire range, from the mountains to the sea, of the Knysna elephants. As I unfolded the large map (which was actually made up of portions of several maps that he had joined together, and is some 1.5

metres in width – I still use the map to this day) I saw that Lyall had made notes and marks on it over the years, and presumably when he was researching and writing *Elephantoms*.

There on the map, at the place of the meeting of the man, the elephant and the whale, Lyall had marked a cross, below which, just beyond the sea shore, he had drawn a blue whale – with spray spouting from its blowhole.

Five years later as Lyall's ashes were being scattered on to the Pacific Ocean at Noosa Heads, Queensland, Australia, a pod of humpback whales appeared and surfaced repeatedly in the turquoise waters ...

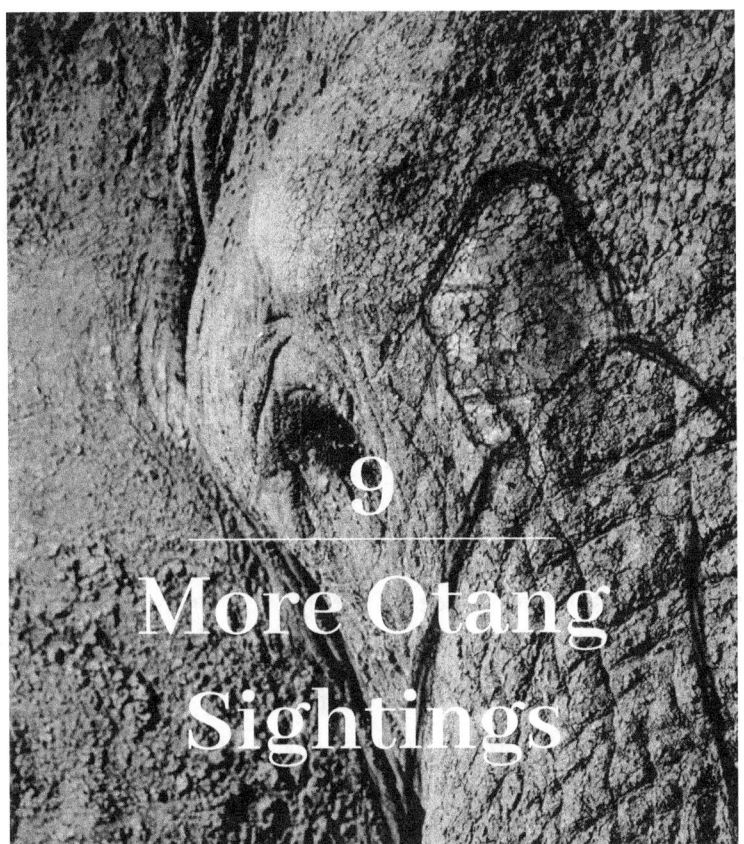

9

More Otang Sightings

As I continued my research on the Knysna elephants and the otangs (keeping my investigation into the latter to myself and Fransje) stories about both these beings would float in front of me, seemingly from nowhere, much like the mysterious beings themselves.

I overheard one such story during the early stages of the elephant project, when I was in the Knysna library one morning. The conversation was between an earnest young man, who seemed to be new to the area and was enthusiastic about the Knysna elephants, and an older man who I presumed had probably lived in Knysna his entire life.

The conversation illustrates how some of the loudest naysayers about the Knysna elephants are at times certain Knysna locals who, without a strand of empirical evidence, 'knowingly' perpetuate the myth that the Knysna elephants are extinct.

The conversation between the two men went like this.

'Back in the 1970s, admittedly, yes, the Knysna elephants were around,' the older man said, 'but they have all died out since then. It was inevitable anyway. It couldn't be helped. In the end there was only one old female wandering aimlessly around on her own. But there hasn't been any sign of her for a good few years now.'

The younger man nodded, somewhat wide-eyed.

'Some of the locals,' the older man continued with a wry chuckle, 'like to keep the story going, it's good for tourism. Every once in a while someone will claim to have seen an elephant, droppings or footprints. Then this might get into the local rags. Funny thing is,' the older man went on, 'these so-called sightings or whatever, usually take place in the season when the town is bulging with visitors. It is a great story for them to go home with. You know,' he stated dramatically, "legendary Knysna elephant sighted", and the fools go home believing it!'

By now, the younger man, the apparent newcomer to Knysna, looked slightly aghast. 'So,' he said, 'you are saying emphatically that there are no more Knysna elephants at all? That they are all dead now?'

'Dead as the dodo, stuff of myth and legend,' the older man said sagely. 'Lives on only in stories, a bit like the story of the Loch Ness monster.'

Everyone has the right to their opinion – but to misinform? I think that is entirely another matter. Hearing the conversation that morning illustrated in a small, trivial way misinformation about the Knysna elephants. Many years later, as I mentioned in the Author's Note in this book, the misinformation grew to the extent that in 2019, SANParks Knysna misinformed the public nationally and internationally on the status of the Knysna elephants. In a well-planned media campaign orchestrated by their spokesperson (who seems to bear a grudge against me, though I have no idea why), they announced with fanfare that only one Knysna elephant exists.

Stories about the otang continued to present themselves to me. Ten years ago, at the time of the publication of *The Secret Elephants*, a lady told me about her son's remarkable, but deeply shocking, encounter with an otang (she had read *The Secret Elephants* and recalled my brief mention of the otang).

The lady was a member of a group of people I had taken into the forest. After *The Secret Elephants* was published I began receiving emails and phone calls from readers enquiring whether they could accompany me on expeditions into the Knysna elephants' forest and mountain fynbos home. And so my *Secret Elephants Forest Experience* was born, and since then I had led hundreds of people on personalised trips into the elephants' home, experiences that are a verbal and visual interpretation of *The Secret Elephants* book. And people really love these experiences.

And it was after one such forest experience, that the above-mentioned lady told me about her son's encounter with what seems to have been a very curious otang. Once again, the story was told spontaneously, without any prompting from me. This is what she told me.

'Earlier this year, Gareth, my son went down to the Kranshoek picnic area in advance of his friends to set things up for a braai (barbecue). It was about eleven-thirty in the morning and, being a weekday, it was nice and quiet up there on the cliffs overlooking the ocean.' (Interestingly, although not, I think, of any particular relevance, the Kranshoek picnic site is only some four kilometres east from the cliffs where nine years earlier Lyall Watson had his magical encounter with the elderly female elephant and the blue whale.)

'He was,' she continued, 'just putting in the firelighters and making a pyramid of briquettes in the braai pit, when suddenly he saw it.'

'Sorry,' I replied, 'he suddenly saw what exactly?'

'An ape man,' she said. 'He described it as standing upright and it was covered in hair. He said it was peering out of the undergrowth near the wooden benches and fireplaces. It was looking directly at him from only about 20 metres away.'

'Wow!' I replied, more than a little surprised at what she was telling me.

'Yes,' she said. 'He was really terrified, Gareth. He dropped everything he was doing, rushed to his car and drove away back to the N2. Initially,' she continued, 'he did not tell a soul about what he had seen that day. In fact for weeks afterwards he told no one until one day he told me. I was the first person he told. He bottled it up for all that time.'

Half-knowing what the reply would be after what I had experienced after seeing an otang for the first time, I asked the lady, 'Why do you think it took him so long before he told you what he had seen?'

'He described being in deep shock for some time afterwards,' she replied. 'He also felt confused about whether or not he had actually seen the creature. I think he wished he had never seen it. He told me that he took so long to tell me because he thought I would not believe him. Which is wrong. He is my son. Also, I knew that such beings might exist here after reading the section on the otangs in your book *The Secret Elephants*. That is, after all, why I am telling you about this, Gareth.'

I thanked the lady sincerely for telling me her son's story, adding that I felt that sightings of otangs are probably more common than one would imagine, but are not spoken about for the very natural and understandable reasons that it took her son so long to tell her of his encounter – the initial feeling of great shock and then the fear of being disbelieved and ridiculed.

I was recently told of another not dissimilar incident (and not dissimilar either in the emotional reaction by the eyewitness). A very good friend of mine, Julie, whose husband runs Knysna forest 4x4 tours, contacted me to say that Jean, an ex-employee, had emailed her to enquire whether she or her husband knew of the existence of ape men in the Knysna forest. Julie remembered my brief mention of otangs in *The Secret Elephants* and asked whether Jean could contact me. I told her that he would be most welcome to call or email me.

Weeks went by and then one morning I received a text message from Jean asking whether he could give me a call. This he did, and so unravelled another fascinating eyewitness account of an encounter with an otang.

Early one morning the year before Jean's brother was driving on the N2 highway which links the towns and cities along the southern Cape coast. Since it was early the road was quiet. He was heading west towards Knysna, with the Kareedouw Mountains to the north. As he was driving he noticed a large human-like figure standing on the embankment ahead of him. He slowed down and watched in amazement as the being (which he could see was covered in hair) ran down the embankment to the edge of the road. It stopped, then dashed incredibly quickly across the road and ran up the opposite embankment where it stood for several seconds before vanishing.

Jean's brother was simply stunned by what he had seen – and (the almost inevitable) shock set in. He did not tell his family or friends what he had seen, until 'prompted' to do so some six months later.

Jean was watching a TV show about Bigfoot one day when his brother walked into the room and saw what Jean was watching. Pointing at the laptop screen showing what allegedly was a Bigfoot, he said, 'That was what I saw on the N2.'

Jean turned to his brother and asked him what he was talking about, noticing that his brother looked pale and shocked. His brother then recounted the sighting. Jean asked him why he had not mentioned it before, and his brother replied, 'I did not think anyone would believe me.'

Jean's brother's encounter with the otang is, I believe, a credible one. He had clearly seen what he had seen. Shock had set in quickly, and he had not told a soul about the encounter for fear of ridicule – until being 'unsuspectingly prompted' by seeing a visual of a Bigfoot on a laptop screen. His, I believe, was a fascinating sighting, and one that should be taken seriously.

In contrast, an entirely less credible otang encounter – but which just might contain a kernel of truth – was a third-hand account told to me by my good friend (and my neighbour at the time), Dominique Diane. I am recounting this story as it is rather comical!

'Domi', a jeweller in Knysna, heard the account while attending an end of the year company dinner party.

Domi is a keen outdoors person and had over the course of a year spent much time with me in the forest and mountain fynbos. Since she was spending so much time accompanying me in the field – and while doing so might have an otang sighting – I decided to tell her about them as a way of preparing her for the shock that inevitably followed a sighting.

So Domi was fairly well-versed on the subject of the otang, and she was therefore amazed to hear the following story at the dinner party.

The narrator of the story had a brother who worked as a foreman with one of the large commercial forestry companies in the Knysna area. One of his workers was known to be notorious for neglecting his work and would take off and rest up when he should have been working. One day the foreman – yet again – found this worker sitting on the ground some distance from the harvesting crew.

The foreman rebuked him, telling him that he would be receiving his final written warning. The worker protested, saying that he was in shock after seeing something terrible. Assuming that this was merely an excuse, the foreman asked the worker what he had seen. 'A big ape man, just now over there,' the worker replied, pointing to a gap between the trees.

'Nonsense,' the foreman responded. 'Come on, get back to work.' At this, the worker pointed again saying, 'Look boss, there it is again!' The foreman turned and saw an otang striding away through the trees.

Shocked, he sank to the ground next to the worker – and this was where the rest of the harvesting team found the two men, speechless and in shock, some thirty minutes later!

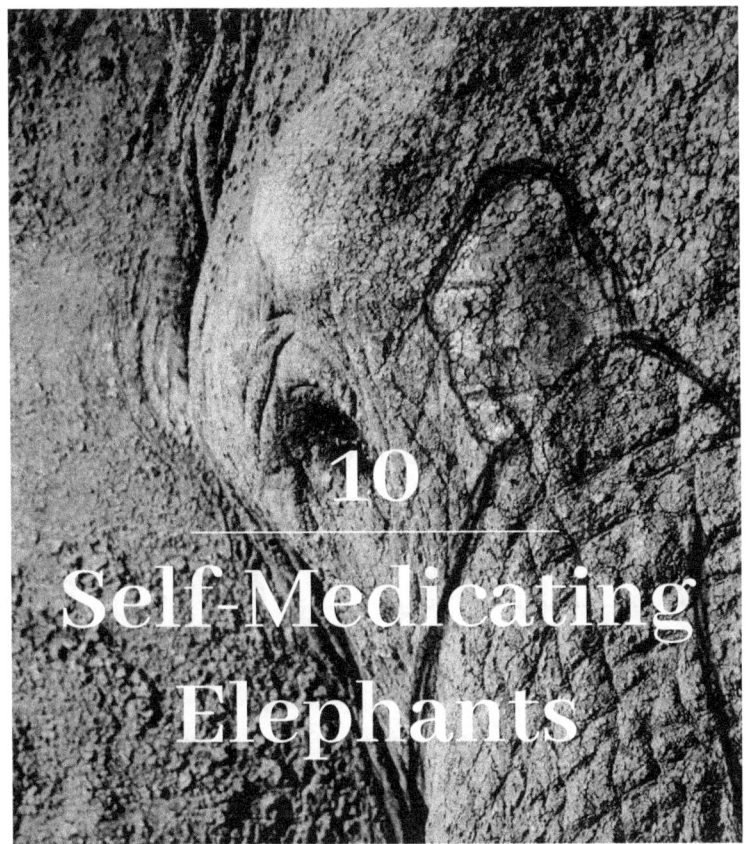

10

Self-Medicating Elephants

Back in 2003 I made two important discoveries. The first concerned the diet of the Knysna elephants which indicated that, remarkably, they could be self-medicating to maintain their health, and the second was that population numbers of secretive creatures, like the Knysna elephants, could be determined by DNA.

As part of my overall study of the Knysna elephants, I undertook research into their diet. By learning what the elephants were eating, I would also learn about which habitats they were utilising.

Every time I came across elephant droppings, I collected a sample for analysis so that I could attempt to identify what plants they were eating. In a moment of inspiration I hit on the idea of using CD covers for 'pressing' and preserving the plant materials of each dung sample.

When I got back home I meticulously sorted and sieved through the dung samples and placed the cleaned plant material in the CD cover. I then marked the cover, using an adhesive label, with the date, place found and an estimation of the age of the sample.

It was quite a laborious process – each 'CD sample' took between two to three hours – but it was incredibly productive in learning about what the elephants were eating and what habitats they were utilising and, importantly, the time of year when they were utilising a particular habitat.

I then carefully studied the CD samples using a x10 magnifying loupe, paying special attention to leaf texture and lateral veins, to attempt to determine the different plant species. Since the CD samples were portable, I was assisted in this task by the expertise of botanists such as my friend Yvette van Wijk and Johan Baard, the forestry department scientist. I also consulted experts such as my friends the forest guards, Wilfred and Karel, and forestry colleagues who worked in the Diepwalle nursery.

Today I have several hundred of these CD samples, with the earliest dating back to 2001. So well preserved has the plant material remained in samples that it looks as though they were created yesterday and not eighteen years ago!

The results of the elephant diet study were fascinating. Over time I identified twenty-seven plant species utilised by the elephants which, when combined with the species identified in previous diet studies, suggested that the Knysna elephants fed on a minimum of some sixty-three plant species. Of the twenty-seven species I identified, thirteen were fynbos species, emphasising yet again that the elephants were not restricted to the forest, and that the vast mountain fynbos areas were a very important part of their large range. With regard to this large range, by 2006 I had determined that the Knysna elephants' range was a minimum of some 620 square kilometres. Previously the Forestry Department had estimated that the 'last' Knysna elephant was restricted to a mere 70 to 100 square kilometres of mostly indigenous forest.

Five of the twenty-seven plant species I identified were alien species introduced from other continents. Very interestingly I discovered that the alien blackwood (*Acacia melanoxylon*), a species introduced from Australia, was present in 54 per cent of the samples. This illustrated that this foreign plant species is a dominant food item of the Knysna elephants.

Early in the study of the elephants' diet I frequently came across a dark brown and spongy substance in the dung samples which was quite different from the other leaf and woody material. For a while this had me puzzled for I had no idea what it was. Studying these brown 'chunks', as I referred to them, with the magnifying lens, they seemed to be pieces of some kind of mushroom. But I had never heard of elephants eating mushrooms, and nor had anyone else at that time.

The answer to the mystery was revealed one morning when I came across very fresh elephant footprints on a forest road. Following the tracks which led on to an elephant pathway, I came across a large piece of bracket fungus which appeared to have been dropped on the path by the elephant I was following. I picked it up and found that it was so fresh that it still had saliva on it. I could see where the elephant's brick-like molars had sliced through the corky fungus. This revealed the cross-section, the texture of which looked very familiar to me.

When I returned home I examined my find closely with my magnifying lens. The cross-section of the bitten bracket fungus, as well as the texture and the colour, was identical to what I had been finding in the dung samples. It was an astonishing and totally unexpected finding.

Through further research, and by sending samples to the extremely helpful mycologist Margo Branch, I learnt that the bracket fungus routinely being eaten by the elephants was *Ganoderma applanatum*.

Ganoderma applanatum is a mushroom species that can be identified by its large, corky, reddish brown fruiting bodies (up to 60 centimetres in width and 30 centimetres in length – but normally smaller) – the very same kind I frequently came across in the forest on dead or dying ironwood trees.

Since I had never heard of elephants eating mushrooms I knew that I had to contact elephant specialists about this intriguing find. The first specialist I contacted was my friend Joyce Poole who at the time had studied elephants for over a quarter of a century.

Joyce had never heard of elephants eating mushrooms either, but suggested I contact Andrea Turkalo, who had spent more than fourteen years studying forest elephants in the remote and wild Dzanda-Sangha Reserve in the Central African Republic. Andrea, I was to learn, had analysed more than 2 500 dung samples – and she told me that she had never come across any signs of fungus in the forest elephants' diet.

She, Joyce and I were finding it increasingly intriguing that the Knysna elephants were routinely eating *Ganoderma*. Was the eating of a bracket fungus a uniquely Knysna elephant phenomenon, and if so, why?

I then switched continents, and contacted the highly respected Asian elephant specialist Vivek Menon in India. Knowing that Asian elephants had lived and worked in association with humans for more than five thousand years, surely it would be there that it would be known whether Asian elephants also eat *Ganoderma*? Vivek got back to me, saying that to the best of his knowledge it had never been known for Asian elephants to eat *Ganoderma*. The mystery deepened.

Through further research, I eventually had a breakthrough. I discovered that *Ganoderma* has been revered as an important medicinal source for people around the world for thousands of years and that it has an extremely wide distribution, occurring on every continent on Earth apart from Antarctica.

I learnt that:

> *Ganoderma applanatum.* American reishi. Like Japanese reishi (*Ganoderma lucidum*), this bracket fungus is considered a powerful immune stimulant and strengthening tonic. There are several known ingredients including ganoderic acids (triterpenes which have a molecular structure similar to steroid hormones), polysaccharides, and ergosterols. American reishi (*Ganoderma applanatum*) and related species of this genus are valued by Aids sufferers for the many reported benefits.[4]

Continued research led me on to the relatively new science of Zoopharmacognosy. This term derives from Greek roots – *zoo* (animal), *pharma* (drug, medicine), and *cognosy* (knowledge). Barely a quarter of a century old, this science explores the behavioural strategies used by animals to maintain health. Today, studies are increasingly indicating that animals do not merely depend on their immune systems, but actively seek out substances for purposes that can be described as medicinal.

For readers wanting to learn more about the science of Zoopharmacognosy, I recommend the pioneering book on the subject, *Wild Health – How Animals Keep Themselves Well and What We Can Learn From Them* by Cindy Engel (Weidenfeld & Nicolson, 2002). It is a fascinating book.

So the question had been raised: 'Are the Knysna elephants routinely utilising *Ganoderma* for self-medication purposes?' I think so. Hippocrates

---

4 Suzanne Diamond (2002). *Beauty in Peril – the Stoltmann Wilderness.* HerbanGram 48: 50-62

said, 'Let food be your medicine and medicine be your food.' An ancient Chinese proverb asserts, 'Medicine and food have a common origin.' In recent times the Knysna elephants' range has been restricted by humans to the forest and the mountain fynbos. In the past they had access to the coastal plains, which today are crowded with development and farming. They even roamed on the dunes abutting the Indian Ocean and on the beach itself. Therefore it is possible that they have adapted and learnt to eat *Ganoderma* to compensate for no longer having access to their age-old full spectrum of food types.

Relevant to this, as mentioned earlier, through the study of the elephants' diet I discovered that alien blackwood (*Acacia melanoxylon*), an introduced Australian species, is a dominant food item in the Knysna elephants' diet – present in 54 per cent of samples. Therefore perhaps it is no coincidence that blackwood is very high in protein (17 to 25 per cent), and carbohydrate (30 to 40 per cent).

Equally relevant, very recent research (2018)[5] has revealed why mountain gorillas risk leaving their forest home to raid eucalyptus plantations (another introduced Australian species) to feed upon the bark. They do this to satisfy their dietary need for salt. As appears to be the case with the Knysna elephants and the *Ganoderma*, this suggests the gorillas have adapted their diet as a result of their range being restricted by human activity, as well as their restricted access to indigenous plant foods rich in sodium.

Most interestingly, I discovered that mountain gorillas also eat and relish *Ganoderma*. In her famous book, *Gorillas in the Mists*, Dian Fossey wrote the following about this:

Still another special food (of the gorillas) is bracket fungus

---

5 https://www.sciencedaily.com/releases/2018/09/180919083459.htm

(*Ganoderma applanatum*), a parasitical tree growth resembling a large solidified mushroom. The shelf-like projection is difficult to break free from a tree, so the younger animals often have to wrap their arms and legs awkwardly around the trunk and content themselves by only gnawing at the delicacy. Older animals that succeed in breaking the fungus loose have been observed carrying it several hundred feet from its source, all the while guarding it possessively from more dominant individuals' attempts to take it away. Both the scarcity of the fungus and the gorillas liking for it cause intergroup squabbles, a number of which are settled by the Silverback, who simply takes the item of contention for himself.[6]

The fact that Knysna elephants routinely and consistently eat *Ganoderma* seemingly for maintenance of health emphasises yet another reason why we must protect the last wild places and their last wild denizens. We can learn from the animals; we probably always have. This reminds me of something Mrs Jordaan told me one day. As a little girl her parents would encourage her and her brothers and sisters to go into the wilds to observe what the wild animals were eating to treat their ills. It is entirely possible that going back to our kind's dawning times, our earliest knowledge of medicine could have been derived from our observations of how wild animals maintained their health and treated their own ills.

As mentioned at the beginning of this chapter, I discovered that population numbers of elusive animals like the Knysna elephants can be determined

6 Dian Fossey (1983). *Gorillas in the Mist.* Houghton Mifflin Company, Boston & New York.

through DNA analysis.

During my research I learnt about the pioneering work of Dr Lori Eggert, a conservation geneticist at the Smithsonian Institution in Washington DC. Lori's research focused on non-invasive methods of providing much needed information for the effective conservation of secretive animals in general, and elephants in particular.

During Lori's PhD research she developed a genetic censusing method for forest elephants in the Kakum National Park in Ghana using DNA extracted from dung. Because the fibrous vegetation eaten by elephants continuously scrapes cells from the intestines, their dung is a very rich source of DNA. DNA extracted from dung not only identifies the individual but also identifies its sex and its relatedness to others in the population.

While Lori and her research team collected dung samples at Kakum, they also measured the circumference of dung bolus (ball). This was done to determine the age of individual elephants. Bolus circumference, research had revealed, is directly related to body size, and hence the age of elephants can be determined.

Small portions of dung were collected and placed in test tubes with buffer (preservative) for DNA extraction back in the laboratory at the Smithsonian. Lori's non-invasive sampling techniques proved to be a very successful way of estimating the population numbers of the secretive Kakum forest elephants.

When I learnt about Lori's pioneering research I contacted her, telling her about the equally secretive Knysna elephants, and how vital it was to know how many of the elephants existed as well as their sex and interrelatedness. At the time my and the forest guards' fieldwork suggested that a minimum of perhaps six or seven elephants existed.

Lori's response was enthusiastic and positive. She felt that the Knysna elephants were exactly the kind of endangered elephant population that could benefit from her genetic censusing methods. She proposed that we collaborate on a population study.

I was delighted to hear this and we soon set the wheels in motion. On the ground, I gained permission from the forestry department, and from landowners on whose land the elephants also roamed, to undertake the study. Lori then couriered a parcel to me from Washington containing the sampling equipment. This consisted of polypropylene test tubes, buffer, and data lists, and detailed instructions on how the samples should be collected, preserved and stored prior to shipping to the USA. As Lori had done at Kakum, I would also be measuring bolus circumference while sampling so that we could age the elephants.

For four months I collected the samples. To be successfully genotyped, the samples had to be fresh – ideally between one and four days old. Of the thirty-five samples I collected twenty-seven were estimated to be between one and four days old and of these 87 per cent were successfully genotyped by Lori.

The results of the DNA analysis months later were astounding. Lori's laboratory work revealed that there were at least five females within the Knysna elephant population. The analysis showed that the elephants were interrelated, with the results suggesting two of the females were a first order (parent-offspring) relationship, with the other three females being half-siblings. In addition to the five females, my fieldwork at that time had indicated the presence of at least two adult bulls and at least two young calves, bringing the population to a minimum of nine Knysna elephants. In addition, the bolus measurements indicated that all five females were relatively young adults.

We repeated the DNA study several years later and found, thankfully, the same five females, plus a sixth female that we had missed the first time round!

When our peer-reviewed paper on the DNA population study was finally published, the results shocked and seemingly angered certain forestry scientists and officials who had long maintained that the Knysna elephants were doomed to extinction.[7]

---

7 The Knysna elephants: a population study conducted using faecal DNA. *African Journal of Ecology,* online version, 2 June 2007.

11

Missing

Missing – lost, not found, gone.

These are some of the definitions of that terrifying word 'missing', a word that has particular relevance to the Knysna forest and its associated environs, such as the mountains and the ocean.

Whenever I hear or see the word 'missing', three cases related to the Knysna forests always flood into my mind – the mysterious disappearance of twenty-year-old university student Rosalind Ballingall on 12 August 1969; the disappearance of a green Bell Jet Ranger helicopter and its three occupants on 6 March 1999; and the disappearance of thirteen-year-old Seteline Moos on 8 May 2004. And I have a strange, although inadvertent, connection to all three of these tragic disappearances.

On 8 March 1999, two days after the disappearance of the helicopter, I was giving a presentation in Johannesburg to a chapter of the Young Presidents Organisation (YPO), an audience of highly successful business people and their partners.

I centred my talk on how, after the murder of my friend George Adamson, the legendary lion man of Africa of *Born Free* fame, I had rescued George's last lion cub orphans and relocated them from Kenya to Botswana. There, living as a human member of the pride, I rehabilitated them back into the wilds.

During the presentation I mentioned that I occasionally used a divining technique, with a pendulum and a map, as a means of locating the lions. This is the same technique that is used to locate water, for example, and geological faults.

Dowsing is an age-old art and is used today in fields as diverse as medicine and archaeology. I learnt about the pendulum technique of divining when George Adamson told me one day how his brother Terence had discovered late in life that he had the ability to dowse and he used it to successfully locate George's lions, and even missing people. George recounted to me the story of a visitor to his camp who had told Terence that she had very sadly lost touch with her son in Australia. She asked Terence to try to locate him. Using his pendulum and a map, Terence discerned that the lady's son was in a small and remote Australian town that neither she nor Terence had ever heard of. A year later the lady's son confirmed that he had indeed been there at the time.

After my presentation to the YPO a woman in the audience approached me. She was visibly upset and her eyes were rimmed with tears.

She asked me if I knew about a helicopter that had mysteriously gone missing somewhere on the southern Cape coast. I replied that I did not.

She told me that the people flying in the helicopter were her friends, the pilot Ian Macfarlane, his wife Frances, and Ian's father Boyd.

She asked me if I would dowse for the missing helicopter and of course I said that I would. At that time I had never visited the southern Cape coast. It was only four months later, in July 1999, that Fransje and I had gone there to finalise the plans for the lion natural habitat sanctuary (which I mentioned in Chapter One). That was my first visit to the Knysna forest, two years before I began the Knysna elephant study.

The next day I dowsed for the missing helicopter. I used a general map of the area since I had no knowledge of where on the Cape south coast it had gone missing. If what or who you want to locate is alive, the pendulum will swing clockwise. As I began, my pendulum ominously swung anti-clockwise – indicating that death had occurred – and it began to gravitate in increasingly tighter circles on the map over a track named Petrus Brand Pad, a place two and a half kilometres south of the Knysna Diepwalle Forest Station.

I did not contact the lady. I had heard on the news later that day that extensive aerial and ground searches were still ongoing. I simply could not tell the lady what the pendulum had indicated, taking away hope when hope still existed. And I then left the matter alone, until two years later when, with the commencement of the elephant study, the matter revisited me.

The official search for the helicopter, involving the South African Air Force, the Rescue Coordinating Centre, the Southern Cape Regional Emergency Unit, the Mountain Club of South Africa and the forestry department staff, ended two days later. Wayne Macfarlane, the Macfarlanes' eldest son and also a helicopter pilot, continued the search for a further fifteen days flying above the forest using infrared equipment. But to no avail. The Macfarlane family, in desperation, consulted a clairvoyant who stated that one of the family members had lived longer than the others.

In May 2001, on my very first research exploration into the Knysna forest, I was nearing the end of the route I had chosen that day, south of the Diepwalle Forest Station. I was totally immersed in looking for signs of elephant when suddenly I began to feel very ill at ease. For a moment I could not understand why I should be feeling that way. I stopped walking. Then I remembered. I was on Petrus Brand Pad, south of Diepwalle – the place where the pendulum had indicated that the helicopter had crashed in 1999.

I shivered and quickly walked on.

Back at home I told Fransje what I had experienced on Petrus Brand Pad, but mentioned it to no one else in the months and years that followed.

Almost five years later, late on the morning of 21 April 2006, a harvesting team was preparing cut-lines just off Petrus Brand Pad. Amongst them was Johnny Dlamini. In the dense forest with its tangled creepers and vines he came across a scene that would remain imprinted on his mind forever. It was at the place over which the pendulum had circled seven years earlier.

In front of him, just metres away, he saw the forest-green wreckage of the helicopter – with the remains of two people still strapped into their seats. Shocked, Johnny turned to run away and almost tripped over a third body on the ground.

My forestry friend Cyril Sam was the second person after Johnny Dlamini to see the crash site. He later told me that on that fateful day he and the harvesting team had come across recent signs of elephant in the vicinity of the crash site. So fresh were the signs of elephant, he told me, that as he cautiously ventured towards the craft and saw it for the first time, with his nerves on edge and his eyes playing tricks, he actually thought it was an elephant.

Forestry employees, people on their mountain bikes and visitors on foot had unknowingly been passing close to the helicopter crash site for years – but not the elephants. They knew of its location and, it seems, repeatedly visited the place.

Back in 1999, after divining for the helicopter and seeing its location in the Knysna forest, I had contacted my colleague, elephant behaviour expert Joyce Poole, to ask her how the elephants might have reacted to the helicopter crash and the deaths of the Macfarlanes. The reason for my question was that it is well known that elephants will scatter earth and branches over their dead and over the dead of one other species – our kind.

Joyce's reply was straightforward and unhesitating. She told me, 'I think the elephants might well have gone to the place and covered the bodies, as well as portions of the helicopter, with branches.'

Joyce had written poignantly about elephant burial behaviour in her book, *Coming of Age with Elephants*:

> If elephants see themselves as different from other animals, is it possible that they see humans as different from the rest of nature? And how do they measure the difference? If elephants have the capacity to think consciously, if they understand death, is there any indication that they can empathise?

George Adamson was convinced that elephants understood the concept of death and that, as Joyce implies, they experience a kind of empathy when encountering dead humans. George had once said to me, 'There are many well-known cases of elephants burying people they killed under branches and other vegetation.'

I have witnessed this behaviour myself. The first dead person I had ever seen, when I was a young game ranger in the Tuli bushlands in

Botswana in the 1980s, was a man killed by elephants. When I found his body, it was partially covered with vegetation and earth.

It is generally accepted that elephants reserve burial behaviour only for their own and for our kind. I have never heard or read about them exhibiting this behaviour towards any other species. That was, somewhat strangely, until an incident occurred just two months before the helicopter was found. In February 2006, while on patrol in the forest, Wilfred and Karel came across a dead bushpig. From the signs, an elephant had clearly pulled and dragged the body across the ground. This in itself was strange behaviour. When Wilfred and Karel returned to the place the following day they discovered, to their utter shock and disbelief, that the bushpig's body had been covered with branches.

Ian and Frances Macfarlane were buried in the cemetery at the forest village at Diepwalle and Boyd Macfarlane was buried beside his wife in Pretoria. Robbie, the Macfarlanes' youngest son, speaking to journalist Nicole Schafer[8] about what the forest had hidden, later commented, 'While it has brought us much pain, it is also a very spiritual place and we are now at peace with what happened there.'

The mysterious disappearance of Rosalind Ballingall occurred thirty years before the helicopter went missing. Rosalind was a twenty-year-old, tall, attractive and well-liked student at the University of Cape Town. At the

---

8 Nicole Schafer, 'Sons at peace after vanished chopper found in forest.' Draft of proposed news article, May 2006.

time she went missing she was studying drama. Rosalind came from a well-to-do Johannesburg family, her father being an executive of Barlow Rand Mines.

Her disappearance on 12 August 1969 is, for a variety of reasons, one of South Africa's most famous unsolved mysteries. Since she came from a prominent Johannesburg family her disappearance was high-profile and headline grabbing. That particular time period in South Africa's history also contributed to the attention her disappearance attracted. It was the time when apartheid was at its strongest, when whites were at their most privileged and protected by the system, and a time when whites' mindset was at its most conservative. Mixed in with this was the emergence of a hippie era in South Africa (of which Rosalind was a part), made up to a large extent of university students – ironically from privileged white families – who were exploring defiance of the apartheid system, and of their parents' values.

Described by her fellow students as being depressed and suffering from anxiety (a state of mind possibly exacerbated by alleged drug use), Rosalind was invited by two acquaintances, Sasja Sergiev and his companion Tanya Geffin, to join them for a break at a cottage known as 'The Sugar House' in the Fisantehoek area of the Knysna forest.

According to police reports, Rosalind was last seen leaving the house the morning after her arrival and she was apparently going for a walk in the forest. According to other reports, she was carrying a Bible and asked the property's staff for directions to a church just south of Fisantehoek, near the N2 main road.

Others said that just after leaving the house, on her way into the forest, she stopped to talk to the white owner of a smallholding with whom she had shared some chocolate. Rosalind's disappearance then – and still to this day, fifty years later – created much and varied speculation. Some of her fellow students presumed she was attacked and killed by wild animals in the forest. Others spoke of witchcraft, and even alien abduction. There were some who speculated that she had disappeared to assume a new identity – in defiance of her family. This would seem to be entirely unlikely as those close to her described her being a loving and caring young woman who would never hurt her family and friends by abandoning them.

The police, assisted by local people, began a search for Rosalind the day after she went missing. This continued until it was called off, due to lack of evidence of the cause of her disappearance, on 26 August. The case was officially closed and would only be reopened if sufficient evidence came forward. It never did, but the speculation continued.

Like the Macfarlanes' sons, Rosalind's parents did not give up hope and privately searched and investigated. They enlisted the assistance of Colonel J. Fforde, a former Northern Rhodesia policeman and, in desperation, they also consulted clairvoyants. One was a particularly highly regarded psychic in Belgium. Using a pendulum and maps he made the prediction that Rosalind's body lay in a deep ravine near the junction of two forest roads, a place less than three kilometres west of Fisantehoek and The Sugar House.

At that time (1969 and 1970), former East African game warden Nick Carter had been commissioned by the Wildlife Society of South Africa to undertake a study of the Knysna elephants. This was the very first extensive study of the numbers, range, diet and ways of the southern-most elephants in the world (and it was Nick's very big shoes that I attempted to fill some thirty years later).

Upon receiving the predictions of the clairvoyant in Belgium and knowing of Nick's elephant work in the area, Rosalind's parents implored him to investigate the ravine west of Fisantehoek. This he agreed to do, but when he reached the rim of the ravine he suddenly felt very ill at ease and, being the wise man of the bush that he was, he listened to his intuition and did not venture down into the dark and forbidding depths.

Rosalind's father died in 1980, and her mother died in 1984. In 1986, in response to the execution of the Ballingall estate (a policy made out in the name of Rosalind needed to be paid out), the Cape High Court officially declared Rosalind 'presumed dead'.

Rosalind had gone missing in 1969, and remained missing.

Missing – lost, not found, gone.

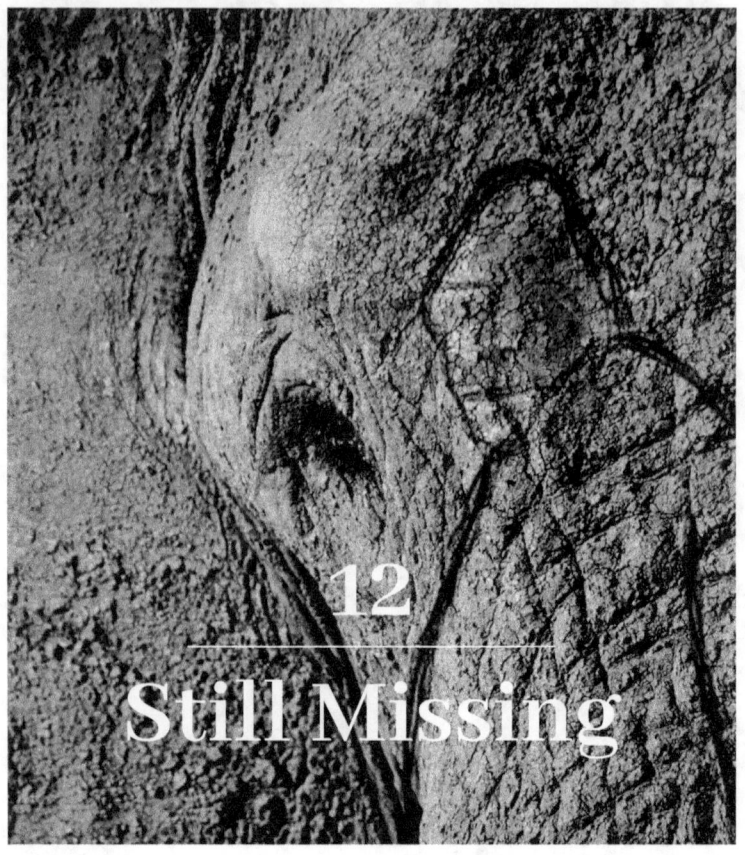

12

Still Missing

ere we fast-forward to 2004, thirty-five years after Rosalind's disappearance. One morning I received an email from Nicole Schafer (who I mentioned briefly in the last chapter). At the time she was taking a master's degree in film and television at the University of Cape Town. As a part of the requirements for the degree, she was intending to make a thirty-minute documentary which she later entitled *The Ballad of Rosalind Ballingall*. Nicole contacted me to ask whether she could interview me for her documentary and to talk about the Knysna elephants and their forest and mountain fynbos home.

The tragic disappearance of Rosalind is a deeply steeped Knysna forest story which I had heard about even before I had come to live in Knysna. I replied to Nicole saying that I would be more than happy to participate in the documentary, and to help her where I could with the project.

In Nicole's own words (from the abstract of her master's dissertation) this was what *The Ballad of Rosalind Ballingall* was about:

The Ballad of Rosalind Ballingall is a recollection of the mystery surrounding the disappearance of the twenty-year-old University of Cape Town drama student into the Knysna forests in 1969. In search of answers to this unsolved case, the film follows Rosalind's footsteps, from the bohemian city streets of Cape Town in the sixties to the Knysna forests, drawing on the collective memory of the Knysna community and students who were at university with Rosalind at the time. In search of Rosalind, the film journeys into the ruins of old South Africa, tracing the emerging consciousness of the hippie era that evolved during that period, partially in response to the oppressive sociopolitical climate of the country at the time.

During the next year Nicole and I went into the forest several times for filming. The visits were usually accompanied by deep discussions about Rosalind. In this time we got to know each other quite well, and have remained firm friends ever since.

Towards the end of one of the filming sessions in the forest, knowing by then that I used a pendulum for dowsing, Nicole asked me if I would be prepared to dowse for Rosalind. I thought about this for a little while and then replied that I would do so, but not in front of camera.

Using a black and white image of Rosalind and a map of the forest (covered with a sheet of newspaper so that I would be consciously unbiased), I dowsed for Rosalind. I phoned Nicole and told her the locality I had found and she asked me if I would take her there on her next visit to the area.

This happened a few weeks later. Approaching the vicinity which the pendulum had indicated we left the vehicle and, with map in hand, set out on foot through the forest to the spot. As we reached the place, the lip of a deep, dark ravine, I turned to Nicole and said, 'We are not going any further, Nicole. Sorry, but I have such a bad feeling here. Come, let's go back to the car.'

Weeks later, during her research for the film, Nicole stumbled on the story of the clairvoyant in Belgium and his prediction of where Rosalind's remains were. It was the same place the pendulum had led me and Nicole to, and the same place Nick Carter had gone to, and immediately left, back in 1969 ...

Unlike Rosalind Ballingall, if you Google the name Seteline Moos, the thirteen-year-old girl who went missing in the Knysna forest on Saturday 8 May 2004, you will find very little information – but Seteline's disappearance is no less poignant, tragic and mysterious.

Since the age of two Seteline had lived with her paternal grandmother Katriena Jantjies in the village of Keurhoek, just ten kilometres south of the Jubilee Creek picnic site where she went missing in the Knysna forest that fateful Saturday eleven years later.

Seteline was attending the birthday party of fourteen-year-old Eugenie Mowers whose family owned a local taxi business. It was one of the taxi drivers who drove the group of teenagers to the picnic site in the forest just after midday.

Speculation exists that some of the teenagers drank alcohol that afternoon. Helping one of her friends out of the nearby shallow stream, Seteline's clothes had got wet and at about five in the afternoon she stepped over the low bridge to wring out her clothes in the public toilets on the opposite bank. She was wearing a black and white Billabong shirt, black jeans and white slip-slops. She was never seen again.

Amanda Mowers, Eugenie's mother, arrived at Jubilee Creek at around six o'clock to pick up the teenagers. The youngsters asked Amanda whether she had seen Seteline on the road as she had not been seen since heading to the toilets. They had checked for her there but, not finding her, they had presumed she had decided to walk home. But Amanda had not seen Seteline on the way to Jubilee Creek.

That evening Seteline's grandmother Katriena was not overly surprised when her granddaughter did not come home, thinking that she was probably sleeping over at a friend's home, as she often did on weekends. The following morning after attending church and asking people about Seteline's whereabouts, Katriena grew increasingly worried and concerned and raised the alarm with veteran forest guard Lietie Sam, the father of my friend Cyril. By two in the afternoon Lietie and members of the community were at Jubilee Creek searching for Seteline. But to no avail. Late in the afternoon the local police were contacted.

Early the following morning the official search began with dogs and a microlight. The next day, Tuesday, even more police were brought in and joined by forestry employees, farmers and members of the local community. This continued until the following Saturday when the search was called off.

Only two possible traces of evidence were found – a slice of bread lying at the entrance to the toilets – which might have been the bread Seteline was said to be holding at the time – and a few footprints which were found on a track in mountain fynbos country several kilometres north of Jubilee Creek. Police said at the time that neither the bread nor the footprints could be positively linked to Seteline's disappearance.

Theories arose that Seteline had been grabbed by someone when coming out of the toilets, and bundled into a pick-up truck said to be seen parked nearby. Some people thought Seteline may have begun to walk home, and then hid in the forest before heading back to the picnic site – by which time everyone had left and the site was deserted.

Strangely, one morning a week later in another part of the forest, I came across a white Billabong shirt and a pair of training shoes. Knowing from the police reports that Seteline's shirt was black and white and that she had been wearing slip-slops, I knew these items were not hers, but I contacted the local police anyway. They belonged to someone after all.

I met up with a policeman later that day and we drove into the forest where I had found the shirt and shoes. We searched the locality for other evidence of the identity of whoever the items belonged to, but found nothing more. Yet another mystery.

When we got back into the truck, the policeman commented on the forest and its beauty. He told me that despite being born and bred in Knysna, he had only been into the forest once before – the previous week when searching for Seteline.

When he mentioned this, a thought flashed into my mind. I asked the policeman, 'Did you find any signs of elephants when you were searching for Seteline?' 'Yes,' he replied, his eyes becoming wide. 'It was quite frightening. We found elephant footprints, their droppings, and where they had thrown large branches onto the ground.'

I then asked him whether he knew that after killing a person, or finding a person's body, elephants are known to cover it with earth and branches. The policeman looked astonished and shocked, and told me that he did not know that. I gently mentioned to him that perhaps the police might want to search again at the place where signs of elephants had been found, specifically to look for mounds of vegetation. But as the official search for Seteline had been called off for over a week by that stage, I doubted it would be resumed on the basis of what I had told the policeman. To this day, like Rosalind Ballingall, no sign of Seteline has been found.

Several months after Seteline went missing I was at the Jubilee Creek picnic site one morning and by chance came across Cyril Sam's father, the veteran forest guard Lietie Sam. As we sat down on one of the wooden benches, we began talking about the disappearance of Seteline. Lietie confirmed what the policeman had told me. There had been elephant activity near Jubilee Creek at that time; Lietie had seen an elephant there a few days before Seteline went missing. He then went on to tell me a curious thing.

As mentioned earlier, when the search was called off, the police reported that 'a few footprints' had been found on a track a few kilometres north of Jubilee Creek – but these (and the slice of bread at the toilets) could not be positively linked in any way to Seteline's disappearance.

Lietie told me that during the week of the search he had gone to check on those footprints for himself, and had followed them for a while. That was until he noticed a second set of footprints had joined the track – strange shoeless footprints following behind the human tracks. Shocked, Lietie stopped tracking, turned around, and headed back southwards towards Jubilee Creek. He confided in me that morning at the picnic site that he believed that the second set of footprints were those of an otang.

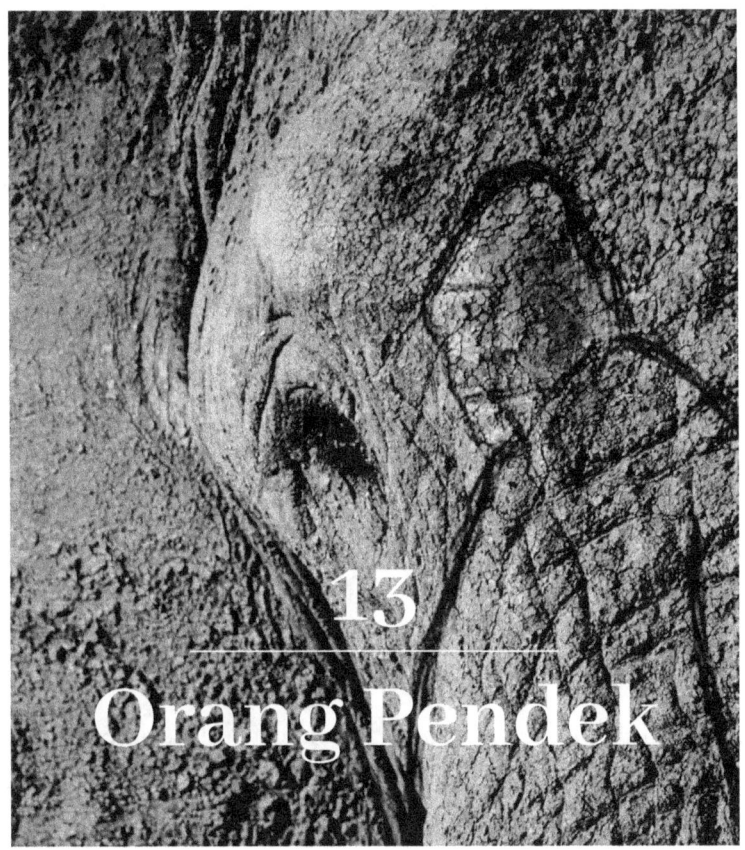

13
Orang Pendek

A part from Fransje, I did not discuss my discovery of the otang and my research into them with anyone else. This was partly because, for the sake of my Knysna elephant study, I had to maintain my credibility. There was such denialism amongst the conservation authorities about the existence of the elephants; the last thing I needed to do was to be open about my knowledge of the otang!

But in 2004 my secretiveness about the otang was to change when I learnt about the fascinating research being undertaken in Sumatra, Indonesia, by conservationist Debbie Martyr and field biologist and nature photographer Jeremy Holden. For a decade, Debbie and Jeremy had been researching a mysterious relict hominoid known locally as orang pendek (Indonesian word for 'short people').

I learnt about their work while reading the book *Beauty and the Beasts* by Carole Jahme, a book that examines the relationship between female researchers, such as Jane Goodall, Dian Fossey and many others, and the primates they studied. Jahme wrote the following about Debbie's emotions after she had her first sighting of an orang pendek:

> Martyr said that seeing the beast for the first time after feeling close to it for so long caused her to cry. She felt a strong pull of kinship towards the animal; it was a relative ...The visceral shock of kinship has (since) never waned and Martyr now feels utterly committed to protecting the hominoid from extinction.

The following is how Debbie described the sighting in her own words:

> The first time I saw it I was so shocked I didn't take a picture. I saw something I didn't expect to see and something so contrary to what I expected. Here was a bipedal primate ...

I contacted Debbie and Jeremy, and an exchange of emails ensued. It was liberating to be able to openly discuss mutual research with fellow researchers. After all, the three of us were a tiny, if not unique grouping – full-time researchers of relict hominoids. There were parallels in our studies. We were investigating a species that was known to some of the local people in our areas, but which was unknown to science. We also had the commonality of actually having seen the subject of our studies. A difference in our work, which I found interesting, was that Debbie and Jeremy's research was funded by the highly regarded Fauna and Flora International (FFI), the world's oldest international wildlife organisation. My research was self-funded. I thought then, and still do, that it was very forward thinking that such a well-known conservation organisation was funding research of what most scientists would regard as a controversial subject – a relict hominoid species.

Debbie and Jeremy's research came about after Debbie, a former journalist, first learnt about the orang pendek while researching a travel story in Sumatra back in 1989. While camped on the slopes of Mount Kerinci, her guide mentioned the existence of orang pendek to her, saying that he had seen it on two occasions in the Kerinci Seblat National Park. Upon hearing this Debbie's life was to change forever.

After a subsequent trip to Kerinci Seblat National Park, during which she had her first sighting of an orang pendek, she returned to England with further evidence – a plaster cast of an orang pendek footprint. This she showed to Dr David Chivers, esteemed primatologist at Cambridge University. After examining the cast, Dr Chivers stated:

... the cast of the footprint taken was definitely an ape with a unique blend of features from gibbon, orangutan, chimpanzee and human. From further examination the print did not match any known primate species and I can conclude that this points towards there being a large unknown primate in the forests of Sumatra.

With this conclusion by Dr Chivers (as well as other evidence), Debbie gained the support of FFI and the Indonesian government, and the full-time study could begin. Jeremy joined Debbie shortly after the study commenced.

Debbie conducted numerous interviews with the local people, and they deployed an array of camera traps in the Kerinci Seblat National Park.[9]

---

9 In the years ahead, Debbie became the leader if the FFI Kerinci Tiger Project. For her achievements for wildlife in Sumatra, she was awarded an MBE in 2014.

Today Jeremy is very well-known for his wildlife photography. He specialises in camera-trapping rare and cryptid species of Southeast Asia. He has captured the images of sixty to seventy species never before photographed including, with his FFI team in 2012, the first photographs of the Myanmar snub-nosed monkey (first discovered in 2010). Jeremy even has a species of carnivorous pitcher plant named after him – *Nepenthes holdenii* – which he discovered in 2010.

I had initially contacted Debbie and Jeremy not only to enquire about their research and to share information about the otang, but also to ask them whether it was known for the Sumatran elephant to eat *Ganoderma applanatum* – the Knysna elephant's 'medicinal mushroom'. I drew a blank with them concerning the mushroom (Debbie thought she had heard something about it from the village shaman, and Jeremy had never observed anything eating it), but both of them were very forthcoming about their research on the orang pendek.

From them I learnt that the orang pendek is considerably smaller than the otang, being approximately three and a half feet in height; it has broad shoulders (like the otang) and powerful arms. Coloration of the orang pendek's hair-covered body varied from beige, russet, and brown (similar to the otang). With regard to diet, Jeremy told me that orang pendek is an omnivore, eating fruit and vegetable matter, as well as reportedly taking meat when available. He also mentioned that the commotion that lower storey birds make when they sight orang pendek also suggests a nest raiding habit. Jeremy had also observed evidence of tuber eating, which he believed was unique in great apes. This was all fascinating information to me, and indicated to me that the otang's diet might not be dissimilar.

Over the years Debbie has had several sightings of orang pendek, and Jeremy has had a single sighting. His sighting happened after finding footprints on a cultivated field bordering the forest. He called his guide over and, pointing at the footprints, asked him, 'What is this?' To which the guide replied, 'This is orang pendek.'

Jeremy followed the tracks into the forest. As he made his way in, he saw a palm swaying. He ducked down and then, no more than seven metres away, he saw the being pass in front of him.

Describing the encounter during a television interview, Jeremy said: 'It was very close. I had a camera around my neck, I was very close to it, but I just kept quiet and watched it, just briefly, as it passed by.' That moment haunts Jeremy to this day. During the interview Jeremy said: 'Seeing orang pendek was probably the greatest achievement of my whole life. Not photographing it is certainly my biggest failure.'

In one email Jeremy told me that the local people would often say that orang pendek can be seen but not searched for. They just appear, as on the day of his sighting. I found this very interesting because this, as I have already mentioned, was my conclusion with the otang. Like the Knysna elephants, otang should not be searched for – but by keeping an open mind, these beings simply appear, as if in a dream.

Regarding my discovery of the otang, Jeremy concluded in one of our email exchanges that the fact that he and Debbie had both seen orang pendek was further confirmation that such hominoids could exist in other places, such as where I was. He felt that the fact that I had rediscovered the Knysna elephants gave credence to my discovery of the otang. 'Discovery' is actually an inappropriate word to use. I did not 'discover' the otang; rather, I became 'aware of' their existence. In modern times the local forest people have known about their existence for decades, and in prehistoric times human beings had known about them, and shared the landscape with them, since the dawn of our kind.

Communicating with Jeremy and Debbie about the subject of our mutual studies was refreshing and, from a professional viewpoint, made me feel less alone in my research. I really appreciated their openness about their work and for sharing information and thoughts with me.

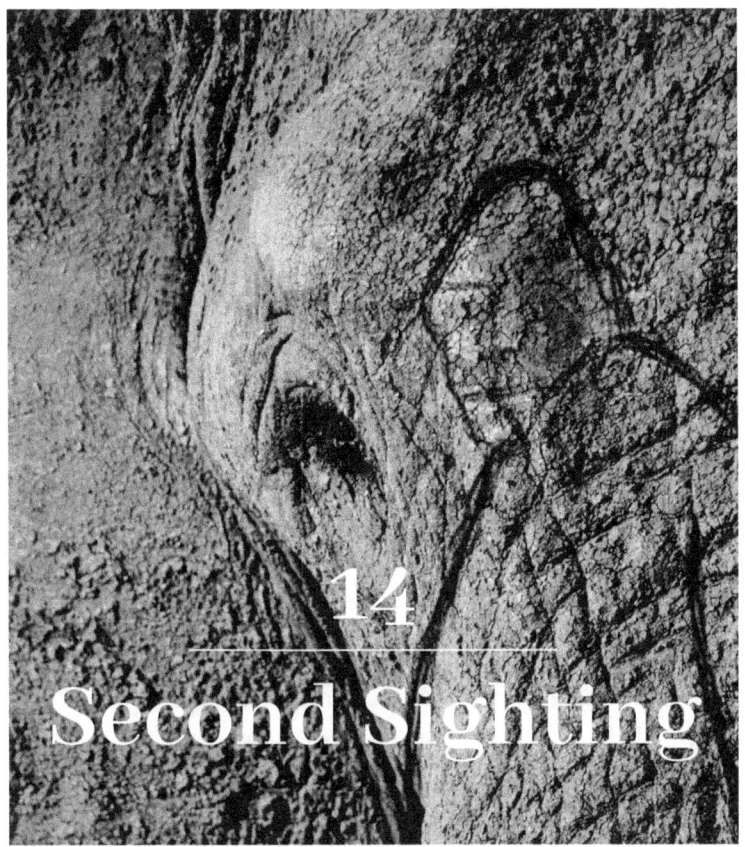

14

Second Sighting

My second sighting of an otang was abrupt, sudden and startling. It took place in mid-2005. Like my first sighting, it also occurred on a clear bright Sunday morning. I particularly enjoyed being in the field on Sundays because the forest, mountain fynbos and the plantations are quiet places on those days – no harvesting teams busy with reverberating chainsaws, and no thundering of logging trucks on the forest roads. Sundays are peaceful days when the land and its denizens (and I) can breathe out a sigh of relief at being free of the intrusion of man-made noise.

The encounter with the otang took place as I was walking along a track some five kilometres from where we lived – an area mostly of pine plantations, but also interspersed with indigenous forest and fynbos.

This area is privately owned by the Geo Parkes & Sons company. The Parkes are an old Knysna family. George Parkes, chairman of A.F. Parkes & Co Ltd of Birmingham, England, came to Knysna in 1891. Learning that a sawmill and a forest were up for sale, he bought both in 1892. Geo Parkes & Sons owns the largest private indigenous forest in South Africa (some 2 800 hectares in extent). Jim Parkes, the managing director, is the fourth generation of the family to head the company. Jim is a colleague of mine and for years kindly allowed (and still allows) me to roam freely, as the elephants do, across their land.

The track that I was walking on that day leads into a particularly beautiful area of indigenous forest and deep ravines. There is only this one track into this area and so it is effectively a cul-de-sac. Upon reaching the forest one can return only the way one had come.

I was about three quarters of the way to the forest, with pine plantations to my right and a tall wall of fynbos to my left, when I was suddenly startled by a crashing sound. I turned to my left and saw it. It all happened in an instant.

View from Back.
Aprox 5½ Foot
tall - Fleeing -

Leaping away into the fynbos – probably less than three to four metres from me – I saw a bipedal hominoid being. Otang! It was approximately five and a half feet in height (though hunched as it leapt away) and had dark, brown-black hair and its skin appeared to be greyish white.

In the flash that I saw the otang, what immediately impressed itself into mind were its broad shoulders, narrow hips and stocky thighs. It had a bodybuilder's physique.

Not only from its size but also by its behaviour, I sensed that it was a sub-adult otang – and I was convinced by its muscular bulk that it was male. Though I cannot prove it, it seemed possible that he had seen me approaching from afar, but decided to leap away only when I was extremely close to him, almost mischievously.

I had certainly received a shock. Who would not, being surprised by a relict hominoid at close quarters! Outwardly I tried to maintain my composure and walked on, continuing along the track until it curved around a bend and put me out of sight of the place where the encounter had taken place. There I stopped, let out a long breath, and thought about what had just taken place.

Then the realisation sank in that I would have no choice but to return on the same track and pass the same spot where I had been surprised by the otang.

Nevertheless, I continued onwards and, on reaching the forest, I went through the motions of looking for signs of the elephants. I found relatively fresh tracks (which I measured) and droppings (from which I gathered a random plug for diet analysis), but my mind was preoccupied with my return journey.

It was not so much fearfulness, but returning to the spot went against my bush judgement. If I had an hour before almost walked into a potentially dangerous animal, like a lion or leopard, I would obviously not return to the place too soon, but the lack of other tracks out of the forest was forcing me to do exactly that.

Eventually I headed back along the track and as I approached the place of the encounter I tried to act as naturally as possible. All was quiet as I passed by, but I wondered if a pair of dark eyes was peering at me from within the dense cover of the fynbos.

Recently I asked Fransje what memories she had of me returning home that day. She told me, 'I remember you being very anxious and excited.' This was undoubtedly the shock factor at play again.[10]

From time to time over the years I have come across what I suspected (but was not always convinced) were otang footprints of a variety of sizes. The most astonishing of these occasions was in March 2007 when I was accompanied by my friend and neighbour, Dominique Diane. As mentioned earlier, 'Domi' was a great outdoors person and often accompanied me in the forest, and she was well versed on the subject of the otang.

On yet another clear and bright Sunday, Domi and I headed out north to check a trail camera I had set up to monitor wildlife activity on the lip of a deep valley. Every couple of weeks or so, I would replace the camera's batteries and the memory card.

After servicing the camera, we headed home at a leisurely pace along a different route.

Just as we entered into the shadows of a pine plantation, I saw on the ground ahead of us small human-like (bare) footprints. We were both somewhat taken aback. Otang immediately and obviously came to our

---

10 Fransje and I amicably went our separate ways back in 2006 but have remained firm friends to this day.

minds.

Using a cigarette lighter for scale, we photographed the footprints (see the photo section). Later at home, calculating the approximate footprint measurement to height ratio (x 6.67),[11] if this had been a human child's footprints, he or she would have been roughly 100 centimetres in height – therefore only about four years old!

We scanned the vicinity for other footprints, but found none. This little individual was apparently moving alone – which was even more surprising. We tracked the little footprints for about a hundred metres along the track before they eventually led off the road and we lost all signs of them on the blanket of pine needles and other vegetation on the ground. We were now almost certain this was a young otang. What human child would be walking barefoot in the middle of a pine plantation, totally alone? It did not make any sense.

Domi and I were amazed but could not think of another explanation. The findings had been doubly verified that day since Domi was with me and she had seen and witnessed what I had seen.

A few weeks later, while in the vicinity of the place where we had found the little footprints, I came across a German couple who often walked their dogs in the area. Over the past months I had met them several times there in the late afternoons. Recognising me on the first occasion we had met, they told me they had read *The Secret Elephants* (in which I briefly mention the forest people's belief in the otang).

As we chatted on that particular afternoon, the lady suddenly said to me. 'Gareth, have you ever seen bare human footprints around here?' I

11 Derived from global mean data of Mietto et al. (2003). Nature 422(6928): 133.

was about to give her a vague, non-committal answer, when she went on to say, 'It is so strange,' glancing at her husband who was nodding in confirmation, 'from time to time we come across these strange bare human-like footprints in this place, some are large and some very small, like those of children.'

One night in September 2007 while driving along the dirt road to where Domi and I lived (and less than two kilometres from where, six months earlier, we had followed the footprints of what we could only presume were those of a young otang), Domi and I had another encounter with an otang. Unfortunately I did not get a glimpse of it, but Domi saw it in clear view in the headlights of her car.

At the time, my good friend Venise Grossmann from the USA was visiting me while on a tour of South Africa. Venise, an accomplished videographer, spent two days with me in the forest filming a video about my research on the Knysna elephants.

After the second day of filming, Venise, Domi and I drove down to the edge of Knysna to have dinner at an Italian restaurant. We had a quiet and pleasant meal before heading home to have an early night. Venise and I were quite tired after the two days of intensive filming, and Domi had to be up early the following morning to go to work.

Domi was driving and I was sitting in the front passenger seat with Venise in the passenger seats behind us. I had my body turned towards the back and was talking to Venise when it happened.

It was an extremely dark night. On our right was an embankment that sloped down to the road, and on the left the embankment continued downwards into a steep valley. We were about two kilometres from home and I was talking to Venise when the car swerved sharply to the left and Domi exclaimed, 'What the hell is that? It has no tail!'

As soon as I heard Domi say those words, I knew what she had seen. I immediately said, 'It is okay, Domi, just drive on.' I then turned back to Venise and said reassuringly, 'All fine, Venise, something has just crossed the road in front of us.' And then I changed the subject, saying, 'Almost home now. We will all sleep well tonight.' Soon afterwards we drew up at our cabins.

I had deliberately told Venise that 'something has just crossed the road'. If I had have told her what it actually was it could have been immensely frightening for her that dark night.

After seeing Domi to her cabin, and after settling Venise in my cabin, I walked the 30 metres or so back to Domi's place. I knocked on the door saying, 'Hi, Domi, it is only me.' She opened the door and I stepped in.

Over a drink, Domi, clearly in shock, told me what had happened on the road. 'It was so fast, Gareth,' she told me. 'A big otang came running at great speed down the embankment at Ollie's place (a neighbouring farm owned by my friend Oliver). It crossed the road in two or three strides and bolted down the opposite bank. That was why I spun the wheel. I was trying to keep it in my headlights.'

Domi went on to describe the otang. 'It was tall, at least as tall as you, if not taller in fact. It was covered in what looked in the headlights like beige hair. It was powerfully built and was moving so incredibly fast.'

The following day Domi was still very much in shock, and remained so for the next few days, despite taking homeopathic Rescue tablets.

Witnessing how the incident had affected her illustrated to me once again why, if people saw an otang, they would be very reluctant to talk about it. Firstly, it impacts deeply on the psyche, and, secondly, the witness would fear ridicule.

As I have said, months earlier I had told Domi about the existence of these beings – in an attempt to prepare her emotionally in case she had a sighting. But despite this, the experience had very much affected her. One cannot therefore imagine the impact of such an encounter on someone who has no knowledge of the otang's existence. Apart from the shock, it would quickly lead to confusion and, I suspect, to self-denial.

I believe I have witnessed this self-denial in a person who I suspected had seen an otang. Recently I asked this person (who has lived most of his life in the same area as I do), 'Have you ever seen anything strange at night when driving home, like an upright walking ape?' I asked him this quite out of the blue as I wanted to see his instant reaction to the question. His eyes bulged and he turned his face away from me, he let out a nervous laugh and said, 'No, no, no, nothing like that.' He then changed the subject very quickly. It might have been somewhat unkind of me to ask him the question, suspecting that he might have had a sighting, but I believe his reaction and body language were very telling.

Almost two years later I had my third otang sighting – and it could have been the same individual Domi had seen that dark night on the road. I mention this because what I saw fitted the description (and behaviour) of the being she had seen. Also my sighting took place in the same general locality of her sighting and in the area where we had found the small footprints.

By this time Domi's job had taken her to live about 200 kilometres up the coast in the town of Jeffreys Bay. We remained in regular contact and she visited me from time to time. Unfortunately (or, in retrospect, fortunately) she was not visiting me when I had my third (and very startling) sighting.

One morning I set out to check one of my trail cameras. At this stage, aside from ongoing research on the Knysna elephants (and the otang), I had established a monitoring study, *The coastal leopard-mammal diversity project*, to monitor wildlife populations and human impact (such as poaching) in the largely unprotected area where I lived on the edge of the forest. To do this, I was utilising several trail cameras. The particular camera I had set out to check on the morning of the otang sighting was positioned on the edge of a deep ravine and had been very productive in terms of 'capturing' the diversity of wildlife species in the area. With this one camera I had excellent images of the local baboon troop, bushbuck, bushpig, grysbok and even images of a pair of honey badgers. Here I must digress a little. How I managed to get the pictures of the honey badger pair, is a tale worth telling.

Several weeks before the third otang sighting, I went to check the productive camera late one afternoon. As I knelt down to replace the camera's batteries and memory card, to my utmost alarm I heard the loud rattling roars, in the dense vegetation just three or four metres behind the camera, of Africa's most courageous mammal – the honey badger! (Its other name is *ratel*, Afrikaans for *rattle*.) These utterly fearless creatures have been reported to castrate animals as large as buffalo. I felt incredibly vulnerable kneeling there beside the trail camera.

I changed the batteries and memory card in record time, and quickly moved away.

Caught on the trail camera that night were great images of two honey badgers (see the photo section). They had emerged from the dense vegetation where I had heard them just hours before.

To return to the otang sighting: I was approaching the trail camera when approximately one hundred metres away I heard the crash of vegetation.

I looked up and to my utter astonishment I saw a large, tall otang fleeing, seemingly in utter panic. Smashing through the fynbos, it dashed to the edge of the steep ravine and vanished. Shock set in almost immediately, but I remember thinking, 'I will check the trail camera another day'. I turned and walked away, looking back over my shoulder at intervals.

Tall. Approx 6.5 – 7 foot high.
Was moving very fast. Fleeing

I had seen the otang (a male, I presumed) from its waist up. As described by Domi, it was covered in beige hair. It was tall – at the very least, a foot taller than myself. As it fled in panic, its head was turned towards me. I could not see its facial features clearly in the couple of seconds I had watched it – but I will never forget its head turned and watching me as it ran. And it moved so fast. It had been a frightening experience, but would have been even more frightening if it had just stood there, instead of bolting away. Its panic upon seeing me was almost tangible. It had not sneaked away, but crashed away.

Later, when I had calmed down somewhat, I thought this behaviour interesting. With my first sighting of what I felt was a female, she had looked at me from behind a tree, seemingly with curiosity blended with shyness. The youngster on the cul-de-sac track had leaped away seemingly at the last moment – almost mischievously. The large one I had seen that morning had fled, panic-stricken. And I wondered why? Was it just a shy individual – or perhaps it had had a previous frightening experience with humans ... Though I cannot prove anything, I think its fear was due to the latter. Thinking back to the encounter on the road almost two years earlier when the otang dashed in front of Domi's car I wondered whether this individual had perhaps even been hit by a car in the past. Pure speculation – but there had to be some reason for the great fear of humans that the otang had shown that morning.

As I neared home I called Domi on my cell phone and told her about the encounter and described to her what I had seen.

She said, 'What you have described, and how it fled at speed, and how it looked, is exactly what I witnessed that night in the car.'

Aftand (also known as 'Adam') was destroyed by a forestry department official in 1971 in what was meant to be a clandestine killing. (Photo: Major Bruce Kinloch, 1968)

Early days of the elephant project. Fransje on the top of Spitskop Mountain, with high-tech listening equipment. (Photo: Gareth Patterson)

Finding, back in 2001, a mass of footprints of three different sized elephants moving together on Kom se Pad (the footprints were of Strangefoot, very likely The Youngster and a young adult bull). (Photo: Fransje van Riel)

Strangefoot, photographed for the very first time (2004) by forest guard, Wilfred Oraai.

The moment just before the sleeping elephant awoke... (still from Wilfred Oraai's video footage)

A still from Wilfred Oraai's (2001) video footage of a large adult bull elephant.

My friend Dominique Diane, on one of our excursions into the forest and mountain fynbos.

With Mrs Jordaan and her son, Booi.
(Photo: Dominique Diane)

Mrs Jordaan with her photocopied sheet of paper
with hominoid illustrations.
(Photo: Dominique Diane)

A still from the documentary The Search for the Knysna Elephants *(NHU Africa/Animal Planet International). Image captured by my filmmaker friend, Mark van Wijk, on the very last day of filming, after two weeks of attempting to film Knysna elephants. The elephant simply materialised in front of them!*

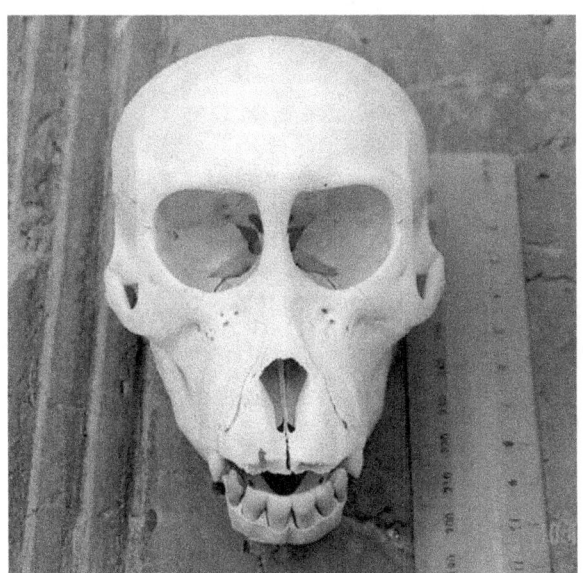

Media photo of Rosalind Ballingall.
(Source, Scope, 23 June, 1972)

The skull of the initially undetermined primate species.
(Photo: Gareth Patterson)

One of the strange, small, human-like footprints I found with Dominique Diane in March 2007. (Photo: Dominique Diane)

Caught on the trail camera were great images of two honey badgers.

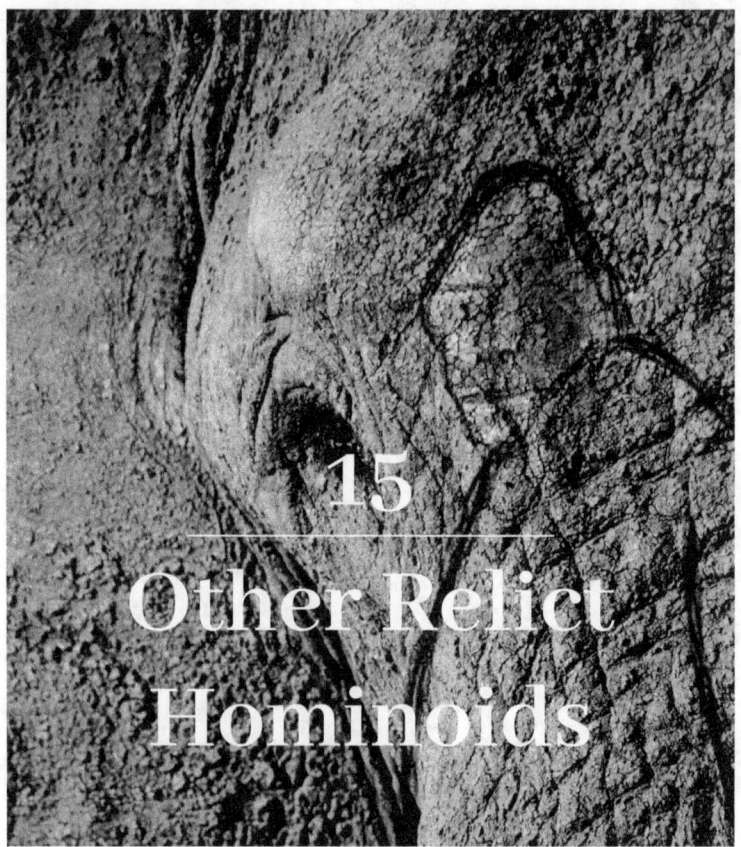

15

Other Relict Hominoids

A year earlier Wilfred and Karel, my forest guard friends, made an intriguing find – the skull of an undetermined primate species.

They found the skull while on a foot patrol near the Rooi-Els River, downstream of the Rondebossie hut on the famous Outeniqua Hiking Trail. The skull mystified them. It was too large to be that of a vervet monkey, but too small to be that of an adult baboon – yet the skull had the molars of an adult animal. Later that day, still undecided as to its species, they gave the skull to Klaas Havenga, the Diepwalle head ranger.

A few weeks later when I was at the Diepwalle Forest Station Klaas showed me the skull and asked me what species I thought it belonged to.

Due to the adult molars, he felt it might be a very large vervet monkey, but was not entirely certain. The skull's diameter (see the photo section) measured approximately 13 centimetres, and it was in remarkable condition – apart from its missing incisors and all but one canine tooth. Like the guards and Klaas, I was also somewhat mystified. The adult molars and the relatively small size of the skull were intriguing. I asked Klaas if I could borrow the skull to obtain an expert opinion on what species it might be. He happily agreed to this.

At the time I had been in contact with the world-renowned palaeontologist Dr C.K. 'Bob' Brain, Curator Emeritus at the Transvaal Museum in Pretoria.

Dr Brain is a remarkable scientist (and a very nice person). Amongst his many discoveries and academic achievements, for thirty years he was involved in and supervised the excavations of the Swartkrans Cave at the world famous palaeoanthropological site, The Cradle of Humankind World Heritage Site (situated about 35 kilometres north-west of Johannesburg). The Cradle of Humankind was where the skull of the approximately 2.1 million year old *Australopithecus africanus* (nicknamed 'Mrs Ples') was found by Robert Broom and John T. Robinson in 1947.

Reading about Dr Brain's work, I had also discovered that over the years he had investigated reports of a possible living relict hominoid known as the 'Waterbobbejaan' (water-baboon).

I had learnt of Dr Brain's investigations into the waterbobbejaan when reading an excellent article on the subject, *Rumble in the Jungle*, by South African anthropologist, Sian Hall.[12] Hall's article is unique in that it is probably the very first to discuss and review in depth the possible present-day existence of a relict hominoid species in South Africa.

In Hall's article I had read about one of Dr Brain's investigations into

12 Sian Hall. 'Rumble in the Jungle', Fortean Times Number 111, June 1998.

the waterbobbejaan, one that must have been very frustrating for him. One day he received a phone call from a farmer in the Mpumalanga province who proudly and adamantly claimed that he had shot dead a waterbobbejaan, and wanted Dr Brain to see its skin.

Dr Brain drove the not inconsiderable distance to the farm, only to find that the skin was that of a samango monkey. It was incredible that the farmer, who had lived in the area his entire life, could not identify what he had in fact shot. Dr Brain concluded that the man had perhaps seen what he had wanted to see – despite the obvious. Perhaps it was also a case of delusions of grandeur?

It was in Hall's article that I learnt that the waterbobbejaan had been sighted by white settler farmers in the north-western part of South Africa since the early 19th century – with one of the most recent reported sightings being that of two boys on a farm called *Leeufontein* (Lion Fountain) in 1965 in today's North West Province. The sighting was reported in *Die Vaderland* newspaper.

The waterbobbejaan is described as approximately six feet tall, bipedal and solitary and it roams the outskirts of farms and raids orchards, as well as reportedly preying on livestock. According to Hall, at the turn of the nineteenth century, members of the Venter family had seen a waterbobbejaan at close proximity, describing it as being covered in reddish hair, with long arms and taller than the average man.

Learning that Dr Brain, such a renowned and highly respected palaeontologist, had over the years investigated reports of the waterbobbejaan was fascinating to me. Clearly he did not fear ridicule from his peers, and certainly did not mention to me that he ever received any. Once, when we spoke about his investigations into the waterbobbejaan, he described his research into them as 'good fun', but he also underlined to me on a more serious note that 'Nothing can be discounted, Gareth'.

It does not take much reading between these lines to know that at the time I was wondering whether the mysterious skull belonged to an otang. Dr Brain was the perfect person to consult about its identification. He was very agreeable to this proposal. Having now being loaned the skull, after photographing and measuring it I packed it into a box and couriered it to Dr Brain.

Generally there seems to be a dearth of information regarding the existence of relict hominoids in South Africa – and this absence of information raises the question as to why this is the case. In the rest of Africa, tribal knowledge of such beings abounds, and (as you will read further in this book) colonial reports also exist. In North America the bigfoot first became a cultural pop icon in the 1960s, while today, as I write, there is such an enormous resurgence in interest and research into bigfoot that it is eclipsing its 1960s status. In Russia and China scientific research into the existence of relict hominids is taken very seriously. Such hominoids are increasingly thought to exist on every continent on Earth apart from Antarctica. But in South Africa, which was colonised for far longer than any other African country, there is almost an absence of information. And I believe that the answer to this absence of information lies in the suppression of information during apartheid, the era that deemed white people to be superior to indigenous Africans.

An example of this is the Kingdom of Mapungubwe. Mapungubwe, the centre of the largest kingdom in the subcontinent a thousand years ago, populated with people who traded gold and ivory with India and China, was discovered in 1932. Its discovery and the findings there were kept out of public view as 'they provided contrary evidence to the racist ideology of black inferiority'.[13] Mapungubwe is testament to a sophisticated civilisation in South Africa prior to colonisation and that 'the findings of Mapungubwe were kept from public attention until 1993, just prior to South Africa's first democratic election ...'

Imagine, therefore, how sacrilegious it would have been in the apartheid era if just the hint of the possible existence of present-day living relict hominoids was suggested. During this era when blacks were seen to be inferior to whites and the San bushman was viewed as 'sub-human', imagine how the possible existence of relict hominoids would have been viewed ...

Possibly the earliest depiction of relict hominoids existing in South Africa at the same time as humans is a strange San bushman painting that Sian Hall writes about in her article. The painting of undetermined age in a rock shelter in the Free State (see the photo section), seemingly shows a 'battle' or confrontation between four large powerfully built hominoids and a party of armed San bushmen. The physical differences between the two groups are strikingly apparent. The (unarmed) 'ape men' are much stockier in body and have larger heads than the almost delicately built San bushmen in the scene. Whether the scene in fact depicts a confrontation between an otang type being and San bushmen is unknown, but the painting certainly seems to illustrate two distinct types of hominoids.

Returning to the mysterious skull, Dr Brain emailed to let me know that he

---

13 Mapungubwe: South Africa's Lost City of Gold. Brand South Africa. 26 May 2017 www.brandsouthafrica.com.

had received the package and that he was looking forward to examining the skull. Then a considerable time passed. One day I received another email from Dr Brain. He apologised for the delay in getting back to me. He said that he had examined the skull thoroughly, and would now like his esteemed colleague Professor Francis Thackeray, palaeoanthropologist at Wits University's Evolutionary Studies Institute, to also conduct an examination. I thought to myself, 'Have Wilfred and Karel inadvertently stumbled upon something extraordinary?'

The next few weeks were ones of quiet suspense.

The day finally came when I received another email from Dr Brain. He and Professor Thackeray, after much deliberation, had finally concluded that the skull was that of a young adult chacma baboon. This explained the skull's relatively small size and the presence of adult teeth.

The mystery was solved.

The field of palaeoanthropology has been experiencing a revolution in the past two decades. Recent discoveries have dramatically changed the shape of our evolutionary tree. Back in 1976, American palaeontologist, evolutionary biologist and science writer Stephen Jay Gould predicted that 'We know about three coexisting branches of the human bush. I will be surprised if twice as many more are not discovered before the end of the century.'

Today we know that the evolution of humans depicted in the universally known iconic image entitled 'The Road to Homo Sapiens', commonly known as 'The March of Progress' (from Time Life's 1965 *Early Man* book) is inaccurate. Our evolution has not been a linear process; it is like a braided stream with many courses merging, mingling and branching away. With the flow of recent fossil discoveries (as I write in April 2019, a new species of ancient human has been discovered in the Philippines – *Homo luzonensis*) our tree of ancestry is increasingly becoming a tangled shrub, with branches of varying lengths.

Dr Jeff Meldrum, Professor of Anatomy and Anthropology at Idaho State University, and editor of *The Relict Hominoid Inquiry* (RHI), described this succinctly when he wrote:

> The past four decades have indeed been punctuated repeatedly by the discovery of additional hominin species ... Today more than 25 species of hominin are recognized. No longer a linear array, or ladder, of succeeding hominin species, rather a veritable bush of radiating branches marks our extended family tree. And even this is almost certainly an underestimate. Conservative assessments now point to easily double or triple that number of species. There is little doubt remaining that the known fossil record grossly underestimates past hominin taxonomic and adaptive diversity. Throughout the past, the rule rather than the exception was multiple hominin species coexisting across the landscape.[14]

And in Africa, according to renowned palaeoanthropologist, Dr John Hawks:

> Africa was full of hominin populations. Each of those ancient groups lasted longer than the entire history of modern humans in the rest of the world.[15]

In short, in the past we were never alone. So why, contrary to the past, should we be alone today?

---

14 Meldrum, D.J. (2016). Sasquatch & Other Wildmen: The Search for Relict Hominoids. *Journal of Scientific Exploration,* Vol. 30, No. 3, pp. 355-373.
15 Hawks, John (2019). Three big insights into our African origins.
https://johnhawks.net/weblog/three-big-insights-into-our-african-origins/

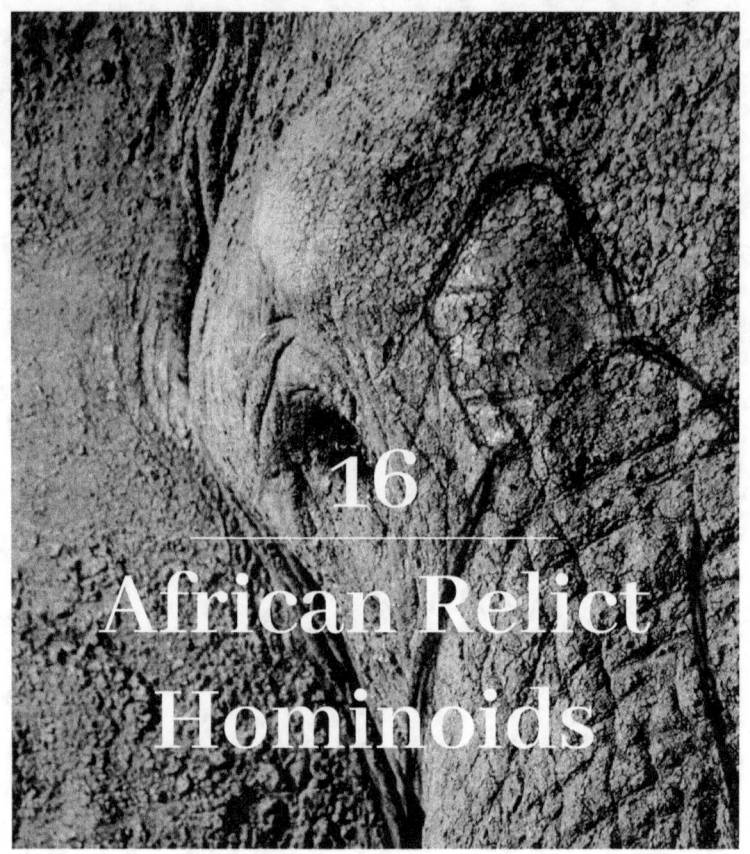

16

African Relict Hominoids

Unlike South Africa, the belief in and knowledge of relict hominoids in other African countries is more commonplace, and eyewitness reports were recorded during the colonial era.

Agogwe, Kakundakari, Fudu, Ogo. These are just a few of the indigenous African names that refer to relict hominoids. It appears that there may be a variety of types of these beings, some quite small, others very large. Coloration seems to differ from type to type and, even as I had seen with the otang, there are differences between the sexes.

Zulu shaman Credo Mutwa, 'The Prophet of Africa' and a national treasure, is a sanusi (the highest level of traditional healer), author and artist. In my opinion he is one of the most remarkable persons of our times. In a 1999 telephonic question and answer interview, Credo spoke about his encounter with an otang type of being in Zimbabwe:

Sir, in the country called Zimbabwe, where I had my encounter in 1959, there is also another creature. This is the most amazing creature, and I saw it once, and so did several other people, some black and some white, who were with me. This creature is a huge creature, and shaped exactly like a gorilla, but it is unlike a gorilla, which often walks on its feet, as well as on its knuckles.

The creature I'm talking about, sir, stands about 8 feet or 9 feet high, and is built exactly like a gorilla, but its body is very powerful. Its shoulders are very wide; its neck is very thick. It is covered with thick, rough fur, like no other wild animal in Africa.

It is a humanoid creature, with thighs and legs and feet, as well as arms and hands which look exactly like those of a human being, only covered with a heavy mat of dark-brown fur. This creature, sir, is known as Ogo by the people of Zimbabwe. And scores of people have seen this creature, hundreds over the many generations.

Some of these creatures have been seen right here in South Africa, in isolated bushy and mountainous places. And these Ogo are, detail for detail, exactly like what the Native American people of the Northwestern United States call a Sasquatch or Bigfoot.

In fact, I say it is the same creature and we have it right here in southern Africa. It is also exactly the same creature but with a totally different skin color, as the one that is seen by the people of

Nepal on the slopes of the Himalaya Mountains, the creature that is called a Yeti.[16]

In Credo's most famous book, *Indaba, My Children*, he wrote of the being he saw as, 'gigantic, taller than the tallest man and as bulky as the largest gorilla. This creature, half-man and half-ape ... stood there ...'

One of the earliest eyewitness accounts of African relict hominoids by a westerner during the colonial era was recorded in 1937 by Captain William Hitchens, an officer with the intelligence and administrative services in East Africa. The sighting occurred in 1900, but Hitchens only wrote of it in an extensive article entitled *African Mystery Beasts*, published in the journal *Discovery* more than three and a half decades later.

Hitchens wrote:

Lastly, there are mystery men-beasts, such as the agogwe, little furry men, which are said to lurk in the Ussure and Simbiti forests on the western side of the Wembare Plains. Some years ago I was sent on an official lion-hunt to this area and, while waiting in a forest glade for a man-eater, I saw two small, brown furry creatures come from the dense forest on one side of the glade and disappear into the thickets on the other. They were like little men, about four feet high, walking upright, but clad in russet hair. The native hunter with me gaped in mingled fear and amazement. They were, he said, agogwe, the little furry men whom one does not see once in a lifetime. I made desperate efforts to find them, but without avail in that well-nigh impenetrable forest. They may

---

16 Rick Martin. Great Zulu Shaman and Elder – Credo Mutwa. The Spectrum (1999).
    https://www.bibliotecapleyades.net/esp_credo_mutwa03.htm

have been monkeys, but if so, they were no ordinary monkeys, nor baboons, nor colobus, nor Sykes, nor any other kind found in Tanganyika. What were they?

The natives of the local villages told me strange tales of them; how, if one put out a gourd of ntulu-beer and a bowl of food in the grain-gardens, these little folk would take the food and do some hoeing and weeding at night, as thanks. That, I can well believe, is myth; but my little brown men were real enough. They may yet be found ... One must not forget that the okapi was once a 'mythical beast' and once no one believed in the platypus or in Tibet's giant panda. Yet all these have been proved to be 'real.' So with the mystery beasts of the African bushveld and forest-ways, they may be improbable, but they are by no means impossible ...[17]

Reading *African Mystery Beasts* in *Discovery*, prompted vintner (wine merchant) Cuthbert Burgoyne the following year to write to the journal to tell of his own sighting of agogwe:

In 1927 I was with my wife coasting Portuguese East Africa in a Japanese cargo boat. We were sufficiently near to land to see objects clearly with a glass of twelve magnifications. There was a sloping beach with light bush above upon which several dozen baboons were hunting for and picking up shell fish or crabs, to judge by their movements ... As we watched, two little brown men walked together out of the bush and down amongst the baboons. They were certainly not any known monkey and yet they must have been akin or they would have disturbed the

---

17 Hitchens, W. 1937. *African Mystery Beasts.* Discovery (Dec): 369-373.

baboons. They were too far away to be seen in great detail, but these small human-like animals were probably between four and five feet tall, quite upright and graceful in figure. At the time I was thrilled as they were quite evidently no beast of which I had heard or read. Later a friend and big game hunter told me he was in Portuguese East Africa with his wife and three other hunters, and saw mother, father and child, of apparently similar animal species, walk across the further side of a bush clearing. The natives loudly forbade him to shoot.[18]

In 1964, Dr George Schaller, who in the years ahead was to become the world's pre-eminent field biologist and is regarded today as one of the founding fathers of wildlife conservation, had written in his very first book, *The Year of the Gorilla*, about the possible existence of a relict hominoid in the Congo basin – the kakundakari.

In 1959 Schaller had undertaken pioneering and groundbreaking research on the mountain gorilla. His findings, as told in *The Year of the Gorilla*, once and for all debunked the myth that these creatures were fierce, terrifying and brutal beasts, a reputation to a large part created in the public perception, almost a century before, by explorer and animal collector Paul Du Chaillu. Du Chaillu was the first westerner to shoot a gorilla. Here, from his bestselling book, *Explorations and Adventures in Equatorial Africa* (1861), is Du Chaillu's description of the end stage of one of his gorilla hunts:

---

18 Burgoyne, C. 1938. *Little Furry Men*. Discovery (Feb): 582.

And now truly he reminded me of nothing but some hellish dream creature – a being of that hideous order, half-man, half-beast, which we find pictured by old artists in representations of the infernal regions. He advanced a few steps – then stopped to utter that hideous roar again – advanced again, and finally stopped when at a distance of about six yards from us. And here, just as he began another of his roars, beating his chest in rage, we fired, and killed him.

Schaller revealed the true nature of gorillas – that of shy, gentle, vegetarian primates who live in closely bonded social groups. His pioneering research on the mountain gorilla created the foundation for Dian Fossey's remarkable research on these animals in the years to come.

In 1966, Schaller and his wife Kay, after studying the tiger in India, undertook pioneering research on the African lion in the Serengeti. His subsequent book *The Serengeti Lion* (1972) is regarded as the most comprehensive book on the lion, and a classic work on lion behaviour, its social system and predator-prey relations. This work was the cornerstone on which all subsequent lion studies have been based – including my own. While writing this, I pulled out my copy of *The Serengeti Lion*. It has no front or back covers and its pages are stained and finger-worn after thirty-six years of using the book.

After the African lion, Schaller went on to study a myriad of other species, including jaguar, bharal (blue sheep) and giant panda, and he was one of the first westerners to have a sighting of a snow leopard. Due in part to Schaller's work, more than twenty national parks have been established worldwide. To date he has written eighteen books based on his work on African and Asian mammals.

Schaller's work sixty years ago on the mountain gorillas was probably the catalyst for his lifelong interest in the possible existence of relict hominoids, an interest that continues to this day. I think that the following quote from *The Year of the Gorilla* indicates his already piqued interest in the subject: *'Wherein lies the difference between gorilla and man?'* he wrote, and he followed with this poem:

> *Am I a satyr or man?*
> *Pray tell me who can*
> *And settle my place in the scale;*
> *A man in ape's shape,*
> *An anthropoid ape,*
> *Or a monkey deprived of a tail?*[19]

Schaller has spoken out in recent years that in his opinion reports of relict hominoids are deserving of serious study, and he has expressed disapproval of scientists who do not examine possible evidence, stating once, 'There have been so many sightings over the years, even if you throw 95% of them out, there ought to be some explanation for the rest. I think a hard-eyed look is absolutely essential.'[20] He also stated that the discovery of these beings 'would reshape our thinking of the status of humans on this earth. People write it off as a hoax or myth. I do not think that is fair.'

In the foreword to Professor Jeff Meldrum's landmark book on relict hominoids, *Sasquatch: Legend Meets Science* (Forge, 2007), Schaller wrote the following:

Large unrecognized creatures may still roam remote forests. The

---

19 Monkeyana, a poem (published anonymously) by palaeontologist Philip Egerton. Written from the viewpoint of 'Gorilla of the Zoological Gardens', *Am I a man and a brother?* From Britain's satiric magazine, *Punch*. May 1861.
20 *The Denver Post*, 2003.

saola, a primitive relative of wild cattle weighing 100 kilograms, was only discovered in the mountains along the Laos-Vietnam border in the early 1990s ...

Humans stand alone – isolated monuments from a distant past. Perhaps we seek an evolutionary bridge to connect ourselves to something closer to us than the known great apes, to reveal more about how we became human. The apes offer only a distant glimpse. Possibly someday the yeti, sasquatch, or some other creature yet unnamed, will help to disclose more about the splendor and wonder of our own creation.

Back in 1959, while undertaking his research on the mountain gorillas, Schaller met a man who was searching for a relict hominoid – the previously mentioned kakundakari. This man was Charles Cordier, a Swiss animal trapper who was reputed to know more about the gorillas in that region than anyone else. He would catch young gorillas for zoos, without, unlike other animal trappers, killing the entire family. Schaller admired Cordier for this.

Cordier told Schaller that the search for the kakundakari had become almost an obsession for him. According to Cordier, the local people described the male kakundakari as being some five and a half feet tall, with the females being a foot and a half shorter, and that their bodies were covered in hair. But, unlike gorillas and chimps, they walked bipedally. It was also said that they slept on beds of leaves in caves and by day, as omnivores, foraged for birds, snails and crabs.

Cordier also told Schaller that he had seen the footprints of the beings and recounted how one was allegedly killed in a mine camp. He mentioned the time when a kakundakari had stumbled into one of his bird snare traps. The kakundakari fell face-forward onto the ground. Then, in full sight of one of Cordier's workers, it sat up, released the snare – and walked away.

In *The Year of the Gorilla* Schaller emphasised that the mountain gorilla was discovered only in 1902, the giant forest hog was discovered in 1903 and the Congo peacock in 1930. Schaller therefore wrote:

> Thousands of square miles of the Congo basin remain uninhabited by man and unexplored. At present I find no reason to deny the existence of the kakundakari.

This statement is reflected decades later in the relatively recent (2008) discovery of a major and previously unknown population of western lowland gorillas in the Republic of Congo.[21] The results of a census conducted by the World Conservation Society (WCS) suggested that some 125 000 gorillas exist in a remote area covering 47 000 square kilometres in the northern part of the country. This extraordinary discovery, coupled with Schaller's statement fifty-five years earlier about the existence of the kakundakari, reinforces, at least to me, the possible existence of relict hominoid populations in vast wild places throughout the world. I think that the discovery of these gorillas (and Schaller's statement regarding the kakundakari) proves wrong the assumption that the world is too well explored for us to have overlooked populations of known – and unknown – primate species.

In a small way this is also reflected here on the southern tip of Africa where, keeping out of sight of prying human eyes, the Knysna elephants and the beings known as the otang exist.

---

21 In recent years gorillas have been divided into two species, the western gorilla, and the eastern gorilla. The two sub-species of the western gorilla are the western lowland gorilla and the Cross River gorilla. The sub-species of the eastern gorilla are the eastern lowland gorilla and the mountain gorilla.

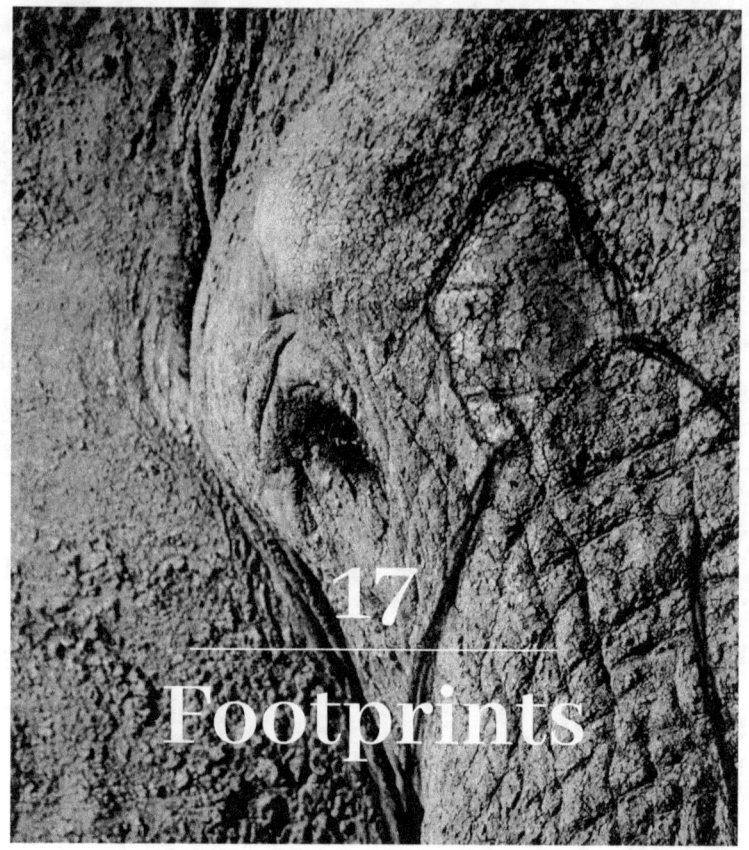

17

Footprints

As I have mentioned, in the early stages of the elephant project it had become increasingly apparent to me that the elephants were not at all restricted to the forest. This was made no less apparent one day when I was following the tracks of a young adult elephant through the forest and up onto the slopes of the Jonkersberg Mountain.

As I was approaching the mountain's eastern rise, the dark forest ended almost abruptly and I found myself in sunlit mountain fynbos vegetation of the reed-like restios, the various erica species and leucadendron shrubs with their conical flower heads.

Following the footprints up the elephant pathway, I reached the rise.

There I had a spectacular 360 degree view of the wild world around me. Below the southern slope of the mountain the forest splayed out like a huge green blanket, punctuated by the crowns of the giant yellowwood trees appearing like heads of broccoli above the other forest trees.

Further south, beyond the forest and close to where I lived, was the patchwork of harvested and unharvested pine plantations some eight kilometres away as the black crow flies. Beyond these was the spread of human habitat, the dwellings of Knysna crowding crescent-like around the eastern edge of the lagoon and ending at the narrow-mouthed Heads where the lagoon's waters mix and swirl with the Indian Ocean. To the north, on that brilliant clear day upon the Jonkersberg, I could see the Outeniqua Mountains, their peaks resembling the jagged back of an enormous dragon fossilised by time.

With the elephant's footprints at my feet, and its invisible presence as my companion, I continued onwards for a hundred metres or so. Then I stopped. I saw other elephant footprints upon the ancient pathway, some large, some smaller, some old footprints, and others fairly fresh. Collectively, the imprints illustrated that elephants consistently and silently moved across the rise. As I stood there I wondered whether they too, with emotions akin to our own, felt joy upon the mountain top. I suspected that they did.

On another occasion in the high country, I thought about the myriad of other life that had existed there for millennia before the rude intrusion, followed by destruction, of the white people some two hundred years before.

The lion, black rhinoceros, brown hyena, black-backed jackal, mountain zebra, reedbuck, red hartebeest, eland, buffalo – among others – were all erased. It was a grim grey image that I held that day, but also one tinged with flickers of light representing the species that somehow survived the slaughter – such as the elephant, leopard, bushbuck, bushpig, blue duiker, caracal, Cape clawless otter, chacma baboon, vervet monkey, and others, such as the otang.

The otang survived, perhaps remaining unknown to the white settlers, but the San people did not. At worst, they were also slaughtered; at best, some were assimilated, losing much of their traditional ways, into the general population.

On the day that I stood amongst elephant footprints on the Jonkersberg, I had not known about the murder of one of the very last San bands of the region that had taken place in 1880 in the mountains to the east of where I was standing. I only learnt about this much later when I asked Janette Deacon, the well-known South African archaeologist, whether the San, like the elephants, might have sought refuge in the forest and the mountains when the settlers arrived.

Janette told me that some of the San might have lived for a while in the vicinity of the forests and mountains, but some of the last of their kind who clung to their traditional ways were ultimately hunted down. Janette then told me about the killing of one of the last San bands. The group, consisting of about eighteen people, in desperation while being pursued by a 'commando' of settlers, walled themselves into a cave. The settlers set fire to vegetation at the mouth of the cave, and then killed the people as they attempted to escape the smoke and flames.

In recent years, palaeoanthropological research has unveiled a remarkable window into life on the southern Cape coast during prehistoric times. The more I learnt about these findings, the more I realised their potential relevance to the otang.

A major part of this unveiling was the discovery in 1995 of what became known worldwide as 'Eve's Footprints'. The three fossilised footprints were found by geologist David Roberts on a ledge of sandstone on the shores of the Langebaan Lagoon in the West Coast National Park, approximately 110 kilometres north-west of Cape Town.

Dated to be approximately 170 000 years old, the maker of the footprints had been walking there at the time when anatomically modern humans emerged.

The following is David Roberts' own description of his finding of the footprints:[22]

Footprints! Could it be? ... Only a few sets of hominid footprints had ever been found in the entire world ... I fell on my knees and brushed the sand from the hollows ... They could have been made minutes ago rather than thousands of years ago ... Gingerly I placed my feet along the impressions and felt an electric link with the past!

At the time fewer than three dozen hominid fossils from 100 000 to 200 000 years ago had been found. In 1997 Roberts, with palaeoanthropologist Lee Berger of the University of Witwatersrand, announced the finding at the National Geographic Society in Washington.

Roberts and his colleagues later discovered a remarkable array of fossilised mammal trackways east of Still Bay on the southern Cape coast (approximately 130 kilometres south-west of my elephant study area).[23]

22 Tragically, David Roberts passed away in 2015
23 Roberts, D.L., Bateman, M.D., Murray-Wallace, C.V., Carr, A.S., Holmes, P.J. (2008). Fossil elephant trackways, sedimentation and diagenesis in OSL/ AAR-dated Late Quaternary coastal aeolianites: Still Bay, South Africa. Palaeogeography, Palaeoclimatology, Palaeoecology 257, 261e279

Among the trackways, which included tracks of antelope and carnivores, were those of elephants. This discovery was obviously of great interest to me as the elephant footprints represented the oldest occurrence of the ancestors of the very elephants I was studying. Dating revealed that the trackways were between 8 000 to 143 000 years old. This indicated that both elephants and anatomically modern humans existed on the same coastal landscape. No elephant remains have been found in the coastal caves used by the humans of those times, indicating that the people did not prey upon the elephants.

The findings of Roberts and his colleagues paved the way for the very recent discovery of a multitude of fossil trackways (those of elephant and lion and other species) stretching a further 275 kilometres up the southern Cape coast. These findings include the remarkable discovery, in a coastal cave in 2016, of hominid footprints (less than eight kilometres from my study area).

Dr Charles Helm, who led this decade-long research, stated in 2018 (in a Traveller24 article[24]) that up to forty hominin tracks are evident in the form of natural casts on the ceiling and walls of a ten metre cave and were made by a number of individuals, *most likely* (my italics) *Homo sapiens*, when the shoreline was two kilometres further out from where it is today.

'This discovery adds to the sparse global record of early hominin tracks, and represents the largest and best preserved archive of Late Pleistocene hominin tracks found to date,' said Dr Helm.

In the February 2018 research paper, *A New Pleistocene Hominin Track Site from the Cape South Coast, South Africa* (published in the

---

24 Western Cape discovers its own Cradle of Humankind:
     https://www.news24.com/news24/pics-western-cape-discovers-its-own-cradle-of-humankind-20180313

open-access journal *Scientific Reports – Nature*) states the following, which in part summarised the paper's content:

The hominin tracks reported here were discovered as part of a ground survey by the senior author (Dr Helm) along a 275 km stretch of coastline from Witsand in the west to Robberg in the east, undertaken between 2007 and 2016 (Fig.9). Over 100 Late Pleistocene vertebrate track sites were identified in coastal aeolianites, and in 2016 natural cast tracks on the ceiling of a ten-meter long cave (Fig.2) (see supplementary Figs S2-S5) *were identified as human in origin* (my italics). In 2017 further hominin tracks were identified in a cave on a lower layer. The focus of this paper is to describe these tracks and to place them in their sedimentary and palaeoecological context.

The reference to '*most likely Homo sapiens*' in the Traveller24 article, and the attribution in the above paper of the tracks being '*identified as human in origin*', caught my eye. 'Wait a minute,' I thought to myself, 'these hominin tracks could also be those of the otang.'

On 2 March 2018, one month after the above paper was published, the aforementioned palaeoanthropologist John Hawks, Professor of Anthropology at the University of Wisconsin, who was a senior research team leader with Professor Lee Berger in the 2013 discovery of *Homo naledi* (hailed as one of the most significant hominid discoveries in the 21st century) commented on the paper, stating the following on his weblog:[25]

The larger footprints are 23cm long, and there are shorter ones that are around 17cm long. The paper suggests that all these

---

[25] https://johnhawks.net/weblog/fossils/late-pleistocene/footprints-south-africa-helm-2018.html/

footprints likely belong to modern humans. That is by no means impossible, but I note that all these footprints are within the size range that I would expect for *Homo naledi* as well.

It might take some time for archaeologists to change their outdated assumption that the entire African Pleistocene record documents a linear succession of modern ancestors. With every discovery, we need to be critical about documenting context and associations.

In 2017 it had been announced that *Homo naledi* was determined to be approximately 335 000 to 236 000 years old (remembering that this represents the age of the skeletal material discovered, and not that of the species. *Homo naledi* very likely could have existed into an even more recent age). With this startlingly young age, it had now been discovered that yet another hominin species coexisted alongside anatomically modern humans.

Perhaps their descendants still share today's landscape, although they are shadowy, and largely unseen, with the descendants of the first anatomically modern humans ...

18

Bigfoot

John Hawks has recently stated that the past fifteen years of discoveries have massively changed what we know about fossil humans.[26] It is no coincidence, I believe, that also in the past decade and a half investigation and research into, as well as popular interest in relict hominoids, has become far more mainstream. The probability that we do not stand alone, and that we could be sharing the landscape with other hominoids, is today being viewed increasingly as a distinct possibility.

As mentioned in the previous chapter, it is now known that anatomically

---

26 Hawks, John (2019). Three big insights into our African origins.
   https://johnhawks.net/weblog/three-big-insights-into-our-african-origins/

modern humans coexisted with other hominoids (such as *Homo naledi*) – and that in prehistoric times a host of hominoids shared the landscape – with interbreeding being the norm rather than the exception. Of this, Hawks has commented, 'What is weird about humans is not that we had genetic exchanges with past people, what is weird is that the past people are not here today.'

Increased awareness from a scientific perspective that relict hominoids exist today is due in no small part to Professor Jeff Meldrum of Idaho State University. It was very rare in the past for scientists to risk their academic credibility (and prospective career advancement) by being open-minded with regard to the existence of relict hominoids. Meldrum was one of the first scientists in the past two decades to publicly state his professional viewpoint on the subject – but not without the questioning of his credibility by his contemporaries. On the subject of bigfoot, Meldrum was once confronted by a colleague who said to him, 'After all, these are *just* stories.' To which Meldrum responded, 'Stories that apparently leave tracks, shed hair, void scat, vocalise, throw rocks, and are observed and described by reliable witnesses. Hardly *just* stories.'

In 2011 Meldrum established The Relict Hominoid Inquiry (RHI),[27] providing 'a refereed venue for the dissemination of scholarly peer-reviewed papers exploring and evaluating the possible existence and nature of relict hominoids around the world'.

The RHI has an impressive editorial board made up of PhDs and other qualified professionals, such as George Schaller, PhD, Wildlife Conservation Society, New York, USA; Ian Redmond, PhD, OBE, Conservation Consultant, Manchester, England; Todd Disotell, PhD, New York University, New York, USA; Anna Nekaris, PhD, Oxford Brookes University, Oxford, England; Jeffrey McNeely, PhD, Chief Scientist,

27 The Relict Hominoid Inquiry: https://www.isu.edu/rhi/

IUCN-World Conservation Union, Gland, Switzerland; Zhou Guoxing, PhD, Beijing University, Beijing, China; and Lyn Miles, PhD, University of Tennessee, Chattanooga, USA.

As we've already seen with fellow board member, the preeminent field biologist George Schaller, board member Anna Nekaris is clearly open-minded with regard to relict hominoids. Nekaris has taught primate conservation at Oxford Brookes University for more than twenty years and has undertaken remarkable work on the discovery of small primate species such as loris and galagos. On the existence of new primate species, she once stated that she very much believes in what the local indigenous people say and '... if local people say something is there, I have a suspicion it may be, even if I have not seen it myself'.[28]

This almost echoes what Jane Goodall stated during a recent television interview.[29] Asked yet again for her view on the existence of bigfoot (a frequent media question for Goodall, who is publicly known for her open-mindedness about relict hominoids), Goodall responded, 'Everyone asks me about bigfoot! (laughing). I have met local people that swear they have seen it. What I find really interesting is that on every single continent, there is an equivalent of bigfoot.'

The year before, while answering a similar question during a radio interview,[30] Goodall (like Nekaris), emphasised the importance of local people's knowledge of species as yet unknown to western science. She said that on a recent visit to rural Ecuador she had asked her translator to ask a group of local hunters a question. 'All I said was, "Ask if they have seen a monkey without a tail". I didn't say anything more than that ...' Goodall told the interviewer. One of the hunters replied, 'Oh yes, we've

28 Searching for the Yeti: Can the Abominable Snowman really be out there?' Science Oxford Lecture, 2012.
29 Yahoo Entertainment interview, 28 August 2018.
30 Kuou Radio interview, 5 October 2017.

seen a monkey without a tail. It was about six foot tall and stands upright.'

Ian Redmond is a highly respected wildlife biologist and primatologist (who worked closely with Dian Fossey) and is a colleague of both Jane Goodall and Anna Nekaris. He is equally open-minded. When he too was asked during a 2011 television interview[31] about the existence of bigfoot (and other relict hominoids), his reply was frank:

People ask me, 'Do you believe in bigfoot?' It is not a religion. It is either a species or a myth. And we need to investigate to see what it is. It seems to me that there are enough reliable observers that see something that is indisputably not a known species, that we should take it seriously.

He went on to state that:

Some of the descriptions by scientists, who are reluctant to publish their descriptions – but will tell you about them in private, are difficult to discount given that it is someone with a scientific reputation – not someone trying to get publicity. Those [descriptions] are compelling.

Veteran broadcaster and legendary natural historian Sir David Attenborough also seems to be open-minded with regard to relict hominoids in general, and the Yeti of the Himalayas in particular. During a televised Question and Answer session on natural history filmmaking in 2013[32] he was asked, 'Is this the final frontier for natural history filmmaking? Is there anywhere they have not been and anything

31 Channel 7 interview at Tyler State Park, Texas, USA.
32 Eden Channel, 12 September 2013.

we have not seen?' To which Attenborough replied, 'I actually believe there is a real possibility that there might be something in the Abominable Snowman (Yeti) mystery', and in later interviews Attenborough expressed an interest in investigating this possibility.

As mentioned a little earlier, interest in relict hominoids has become increasingly mainstream in the last decade and a half and in the last few years in particular I have witnessed a surge of public interest in beings such as bigfoot, the yeti, orang pendek and the Australian yowie. This is due in no small part to the hugely popular Animal Planet reality show *Finding Bigfoot*. The show ran for nine seasons, some ninety episodes, between 2011 and 2018 and followed researchers Matt Moneymaker, James 'Bobo' Fay, Cliff Barackman, and sceptic scientist Ranae Holland on their travels in search of relict hominoids across North America (and in later episodes in Southeast Asia, South America, Australia and the UK).

It is often joked that *Finding Bigfoot* never actually found bigfoot (in truth, how could they, when accompanied by a whole production team in the wilds?), but the show (with its high ratings) certainly stimulated great worldwide interest in the relict hominoid phenomenon in a very entertaining way.

Not since the release of the iconic 1967 Patterson-Gimlin film of a bigfoot, popularly dubbed 'Patty', have relict hominoids fired up so much public interest. The Patterson-Gimlin film is said to be the most scrutinised footage of film ever after the 8mm footage (known as the 'Zapruder film') of the 1963 assassination of President John F. Kennedy. The Patterson-Gimlin film, which runs for almost a minute and was shot alongside Bluff Creek in Northern California, has never been debunked despite being intensely scrutinised over the past fifty-two years by scientists, film analysts, special effects experts and forensic specialists. To people like Jeff Meldrum, the film sets such a high bar of proof of the existence of bigfoot that it has not been matched to this day.

The extraordinary footage was filmed by Bigfoot investigator Roger Patterson (no relation) while accompanied by Robert 'Bob' Gimlin.

164

Frame 352 of the film shows the estimated six to seven foot tall bigfoot (identified as being a female due to prominent breasts) turning her head in the direction of the camera, as she paces away.[33]

Ian Redmond made an interesting observation about the film while asserting why he thought the footage is compelling and not a hoax. Ian, a mountain gorilla expert, said in an interview:

> The back of this creature (Patty) is not dissimilar to (that) of a silverback (mountain gorilla), but back in 1967 there was only one book, George Schaller's book, on mountain gorillas and no good film footage, nothing you could base your model on if you were trying to mock up a costume. Therefore I find it a very compelling bit of footage.

Similarly, Jeff Meldrum once said, '... images of great apes show many of those features (of Patty)', concluding that (and remember that he is a professor of anatomy and anthropology), 'On the basis of the feet and footprints alone, I am convinced that it is an authentic piece of film footage. When you add all that goes with it, it is an overwhelmingly convincing case, I believe.'

As mentioned, the series *Finding Bigfoot* (among others) contributed greatly towards the current public interest in relict hominoids, as did the Patterson-Gimlin film in the 1960s. In the past few years, citizen scientists on the subject have emerged worldwide, some of whom have gained public popularity and followings through their very informative and entertaining YouTube channels. There is Bigfoot Tony and ThinkerThunker who do excellent 'breakdowns' and analyses of video footage (taken by the public and posted on the internet) of what might, or might not, be relict hominoids.

---

33 To view the Patterson-Gimlin film in unprecedented clarity – enhanced by bigfoot researcher M.K. Davis – see the following YouTube link: https://www.youtube.com/watch?v=ngVH-7tMp-jo

There is Andy McGrath and his Beastly Theories, and Bigfoot Odyssey, who undertake thoroughly interesting interviews with cryptozoology researchers about their investigations and findings. Others, such as Justin Chernipeski of Mountain Beast Mysteries, Christopher Noel of Impossible Visits and Mattsquatch Presents, not only post intriguing features about relict hominoids, but also produce and post documentaries of their own explorations into the wilds. I believe that citizen scientists such as these are providing a great public service as, in an entertaining way, they are creating awareness and communication on the subject. I for one have learnt much from these channels.

Creating communication and discourse through their channels also has a therapeutic value. I have mentioned several times in this book the debilitating shock that can follow a relict hominoid sighting. This is certainly a form of post-traumatic stress disorder (PTSD). Host Kerry Arnold of Bigfoot Odyssey, who has himself suffered the shock and stress caused by seeing a relict hominoid, discusses this and encourages fellow sufferers to talk about their encounters.

This is most important. Sightings are much more common than reported, but people are reluctant to talk about them for fear of ridicule, not even telling family or close friends. And therefore they live in a lonely damaging cocoon. Speaking about their sightings, and sharing them with other 'encounters', relieves this isolation.

Believe me, at the end of the day you do not want to see one of these beings. Some people have afterwards avoided going into the wilds and, if they live close to the wilds, cannot leave a window open at night. Their (not everyone of course, but many) lifestyles are changed. So having an avenue to talk about their experiences and their effects is very important; it enables them to understand that they are not alone. Hats off to Kerry Arnold for providing this public service.[34]

---

34 Tragically, Kerry Arnold passed away in 2022.

San Bushman painting of a 'confrontation' between large, powerfully built hominoids, and a party of armed San bushmen. (Photo: H.C. Woodhouse, 1979)

With my good friend Wilfred Oraai. (Photo: Judith Von Prockl-Stadler)

Jane Goodall is publicly known for her open-mindedness about the existence of relict hominoids. (Photo: Kate Stephenson)

Trail camera photograph of a leopard in 'leopard gorge'.

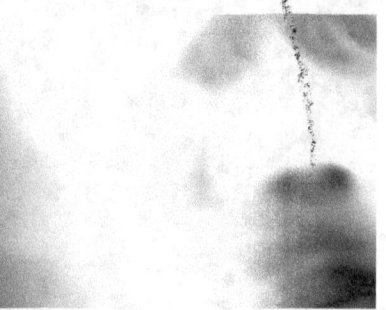

Otang? No, an inquisitive baboon investigating the trail camera.

Leading a Secret Elephant Forest Experience with guests.
(Photo: Daniela Johnen)

My bush dog Tuli, who I sorely miss.

Terrifying! The 2017 Knysna wildfires that almost engulfed us. Photo taken close to our cabins, by Arnaud de Groot.

My Asian elephant expert friend Petra who, with my brother Stewart, undertook the second (2009) DNA census with me. Petra is also an otang eyewitness.
(Photo: Stewart Patterson)

Aftermath of the 2017 Knysna wildfires. A forest buzzard launches itself upwards like the proverbial phoenix from the ashes. (Photo: Gareth Patterson)

Happy to have found signs that two of the elephants had moved ahead of the 2018 mountain wildfires, and found safety in the forest. (Photo: Christa le Roux)

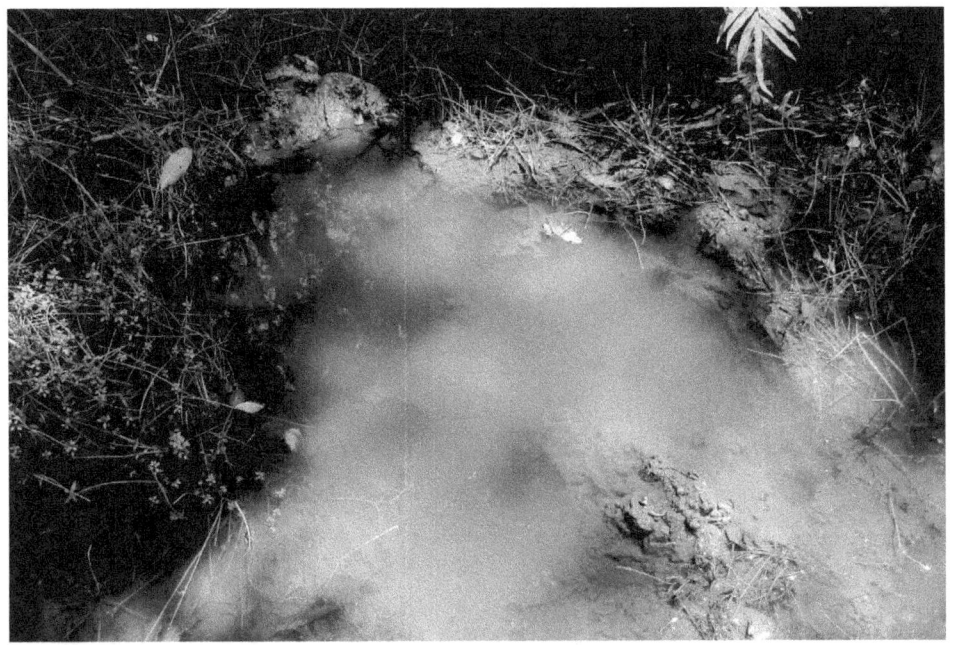

'Their footprints were smudged into a large mud puddle.' (Photo: Christa le Roux)

19

Tuli

For almost a decade my constant companion on excursions into the wilds, looking for signs of the otang, was my bush dog Tuli. We shared many extraordinary adventures together, involving not only otang, but leopard, baboon, honey badger, venomous snakes, and terrifying wildfires. Hers was an eventful life. Sadly, Tuli passed away in July 2018.

Tuli was found, just days old and covered in ticks, by my rhino researcher friend Jed Bird on the boundary of the Addo Elephant National Park. How she became my loyal and seasoned comrade in arms in the wilds is a curious story.

Many years before Tuli was born and as Jed was about to complete his schooling in Knysna, his mother Debbie, an acquaintance of mine, approached me one day to ask whether I would mentor Jed on weekends on my field trips in the forest and mountain fynbos. Having met Jed previously, I had sensed that he was imbued with a dedication to wildlife and to the environment in general.

Out in the wilds together, Jed often asked me about my life with the Adamson lions in the Tuli bushlands in Botswana. The name 'Tuli' became embedded in Jed's mind.

Years later, when he found the close-to-death puppy, he named her Tuli and with Jordana, his partner at the time, they somehow managed to nurse her back to health. Tuli lived with Jed and Jordana at Addo Elephant National Park for almost seven months. Then the day came when Jed was offered the opportunity of becoming a rhino researcher in the world famous Hluhluwe-iMfolozi Game Reserve in KwaZulu-Natal. This was a great opportunity for him, but there was a policy of 'no dogs allowed'. It was then that I received a phone call from Jed asking, 'Would you consider taking on my young bush dog, Gareth? Her name is Tuli.'

With a name like that, I could hardly refuse. And my last animal companion, a little spaniel named Fabian who I had adopted years earlier, had passed away the year before.

I learnt from Jed that Tuli was a free spirit. At Addo, he, Jordana and Tuli lived in a fenced staff accommodation compound and each morning Tuli would enthusiastically visit each and every staff quarter – and its occupants. Tuli was loved by all. When she came to live with me, she maintained this routine of 'going visiting' (often to my exasperation, as where I live is unfenced), right up until the year before she died. Tuli even went 'walk-about' before Jed could deliver her to me.

Several days prior to bringing Tuli to me, she went missing. Jed was staying with his parents when Tuli slipped out of the garden one morning.

At the time Jed feared she would never be seen again. He and Jordana put up notices in all the local veterinary clinics as well as in the local newspapers, and searched the Knysna suburbs and surrounding townships.

Eventually someone in a township recognised Tuli from the picture in a leaflet Jed had been handing out. She had been seen on a makeshift string leash with a young man. Jed managed to track the man down and he said that, yes, he had found Tuli wandering, but the day before he had sold her to a friend of his! The friend (and Tuli) were found and Tuli was 'sold' back to Jed for the same price she had been bought for. And very soon afterwards Tuli was brought to my cabin, and my life with her began.

Tuli was an *Africanis*, the type known as the original aboriginal dog of subequatorial Africa, native dogs whose heritage goes back some seven thousand years. Brought south by early Iron Age Bantu herders, Tuli's kind are known for their even temperaments, bravery, loyalty, friendliness, great stamina and extremely robust health. In her entire life Tuli went to the vet only for inoculations, to be spayed and, finally, almost a decade later to be put down when illness finally caught up with her. Otherwise, she did not have a sick day in her entire life.

The *Africanis* is truly the Dog of Africa, and therefore she and I were perfect companions. As well as sharing encounters with otang, leopard and honey badger, we had close shaves on three occasions with puff adders. The two brief encounters with what I am certain were otang took place on both occasions when we were accompanied on field explorations by my elephant research colleague Petra ten Velde. Petra, a wildlife biologist, is an Asian elephant expert who, with my brother Stewart, undertook the second (2009) DNA elephant census with me.

The first encounter took place several months after Tuli came to live with me. The three of us set out north on foot from my cabin to explore the south-eastern portion of the elephants' range. It was a lengthy walk covering some 25 kilometres. We arrived back at the cabin in the afternoon a little fatigued, but to our astonishment Tuli seemed as fresh as when she started the day – such is the energy and stamina of these kinds of dogs.

That day we had been successful in finding signs of the elephants. We measured footprints and dung circumference and also gathered dung samples for later analysis. We had been pleased with our findings and headed unhurriedly southwards in the direction of home. The route took us through the place where some four and a half years earlier I had had the encounter with what I presumed was a sub-adult otang.

As we passed through the area we were alerted by a sound and turning around I saw, very fleetingly, some seventy metres away, a seemingly upright figure dashing through a swath of young eucalyptus trees which were approximately eight to nine feet tall. Because of the upright posture and the height of what we had seen, I was fairly confident that it was an otang. Neither bushpig nor bushbuck could have created the disturbance at that height. Whoever or whatever had sped through the trees must have been about five feet tall.

I looked down at Tuli. She was staring with a serious expression in the direction of what we had heard and then fleetingly seen. As a precaution I put Tuli on her leash, and after a brief discussion with Petra on what we had encountered, we moved back towards the place where we had seen the movements. I must admit to feeling a little trepidation as we moved towards and along the side of the young eucalyptus trees and Petra later confirmed that she had experienced a similar sensation. I felt that we were being watched. Tuli was silent, serious and alert. After a short while we moved away from the place, with Tuli occasionally turning to look back at it, a mannerism I would see repeated many times over the years.

Recently (September 2019), I contacted Petra to check the facts of the encounter and to ask her what she remembered of it. Her answers were astounding. All these years later I had not realised that she had, in fact, had a clear sighting of an otang that day. She replied:

> What I remember most from that first episode, is that we heard something, we turned around, and for a fleeting moment we were looking straight at a creature that was upright, and then it was gone as though it had just been a mirage. I can still see the image – it was almost like looking at what I can imagine it would be to be looking at a short upright gorilla ... I remember feeling quite sort of 'creeped out', for lack of a better word, and certainly wouldn't have felt that way with a baboon. It was the swiftness of movement – and that on two legs.

The excitement – and the shock – was not over for the day. When we reached the edge of a plantation that had burnt in a wildfire some months earlier, we knelt down to examine the fynbos species emerging from the still blackened surface of the ground. Tuli looked on questioningly.

As I was gliding my hand over the surface of the ground, my fingers touched something smooth and cool – and it moved rapidly under my hand. I yelled in shock and in a flash, the three of us bolted backwards, with Petra and I rapidly getting back on our feet.

A large yellow Cape cobra slithered away in front of us. It was the very first Cape cobra I had ever seen in the area; in fact, it was the first I had ever seen in my life! And I had inadvertently placed my fingers on it...

It is said that, with the black mamba, the Cape cobra accounts for the majority of fatal snake bites in South Africa.

The second otang encounter that I had while accompanied by Petra and Tuli occurred one day when we were walking down into a dark valley four kilometres from my cabin which I had named 'leopard gorge'. We were going there to change the batteries and memory card of a trail camera I had set up there close to a fast flowing stream. It was at this place a few months earlier that the trail camera had captured an extraordinary image of a leopard in broad daylight, at almost midday on a cool winter's day (see the photo section). The leopard had walked up to the camera and, as the image shows, apparently rubbed against it and the small tree that it was attached to.

Tuli was always watchful and alert when we went down into leopard gorge (and for very good reason), but on that particular day with Petra she was noticeably more alert and I wondered if an otang was the reason for this. I felt unusually edgy too.

As always when entering leopard gorge, I had put Tuli on her lead. Petra held her as I changed the cameras batteries and exchanged memory cards. We then decided to walk a short distance up the opposite side of leopard gorge from the way we had come.

Then it happened. Ahead and above us on an embankment, at approximate human height, a figure dashed away, breaking branches as it ran and snapping twigs underfoot. Its flight definitely sounded bipedal and human-like and for a moment I was almost convinced it was a person, and almost called out. Then there was silence.

Because of the height, this was no bushbuck or bushpig dashing away from us. Whatever it was, it ran in a panicked manner, just as the tall otang had fled from me two years earlier and disappeared down into (perhaps by no coincidence) the very same gorge that we were in that morning.

Cautiously, I moved ahead of Petra and Tuli to investigate further. Although I now thought it was unlikely to be a person, I was not totally convinced. But I saw nothing that could confirm or deny whether or not it was a person. Why I thought it was unlikely to be a person was that human activity in the gorge is almost always restricted to the track we were on, and not the steep embankment above the road. I would occasionally encounter pick-up trucks on the track with Jim Parke's workers trundling up to work in the plantations, or heading home at the end of the day. Over weekends I might occasionally also come across people on their mountain bikes, or a runner or two, but always on the track and certainly not in the thick tangle of vegetation on both sides of the gorge road.

I moved back to Petra and Tuli and said, 'I cannot see anything, but I am not comfortable with this, Petra. Let's head back.' Petra nodded. As we headed away, Tuli, as she did on the previous occasion, repeatedly looked behind her until we were some distance from where the encounter had occurred.

On the subject of trail cameras, Tuli and I were to have several other mysterious incidents in the vicinity of leopard gorge. Once, with Domi Diane, we secured a trail camera firmly with straps between exposed tree roots, up on an embankment overlooking the gorge track. It seemed the perfect set-up to capture the images of anything heading down to a low concrete causeway that links the gorge track across the stream.

When checking on the camera a few days later, I found to my utter surprise that it had been violently ripped out and was lying several metres away on the edge of the track. Even more surprising and strange was that, when checking the memory card, there were no images of the culprit who had dislodged the camera. In the past I have had a few trail cameras stolen by poachers hunting with dogs. Knowing that the images could incriminate them, poachers simply unstrapped the camera and went off with it – with me returning a few days later to discover, frustratingly, that the camera was missing. The footprints of the poachers and the pugmarks of their dogs always betrayed their presence in the vicinity.

Needless to say, when I found the camera had been dislodged and flung to the ground I knew that it was not the work of poachers who, on occasion, having not detected my cameras, have been caught in images showing them passing by with their hunting dogs.

Another mysterious incident with Tuli occurred in the upper reaches of leopard gorge. Again, I had very securely attached a camera to an embankment. To do this thoroughly takes time and I remember how on that occasion Tuli grew bored with her inactivity (she was leashed to a tree) as I concentrated on securing the camera, and that she fidgeted and even whined.

One evening, several days later, I returned to check on the trail camera with Tuli. I found the camera still very firmly secured, but it had been partly obscured by loose soil, leaves and twigs. When I got back home and checked the memory card, it showed several images of bushbuck passing by, but nothing to indicate what had placed the soil and vegetation on and around the camera.

A rational explanation of the earlier dislodged trail camera would be baboons – but this does not explain the fact that the memory card did not show them to be the perpetrators. On numerous other occasions my trail cameras have captured images of baboons, at times extremely close as they examined cameras (see the photo section). Again the lack of images does not explain how baboons could have placed the soil and leaves on the camera on the second occasion. Another factor to take into account is that when baboon troops move through an area they leave behind much evidence of their presence, such as tracks, droppings and feeding signs, none of which I had found on either of these occasions.

So these two incidents involving the trail cameras, in an area of known otang activity, was mysterious and baffling.

It is interesting and intriguing that in North America where literally hundreds of thousands of trail cameras are deployed by hunters, wildlife enthusiasts and bigfoot researchers every year, none have ever clearly captured an image of a bigfoot. Jeremy and Debbie's numerous placements of trail cameras for a decade and a half failed to capture images of orang pendek – yet had captured images of elusive tigers, deer and other secretive creatures. And the same applies to my placement of cameras over many years regarding the otang. No images of relict hominoids. The question is, why is this? I believe that they are simply aware of the cameras as something alien to their environment (in what is their familiar 'backyard') and are wary of them. These are intelligent beings.

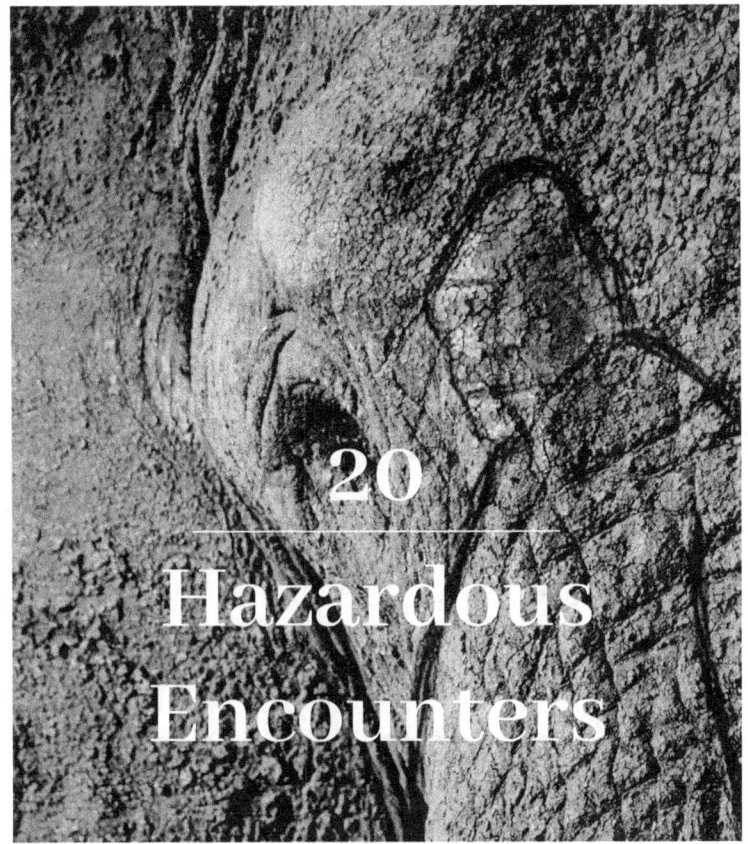

20

Hazardous Encounters

I am certain that Tuli, with her extremely keen sight and sense of smell, must have, compared to me, been aware of the presence of otang on many occasions on our explorations. I feel that the occasions when we encountered leopard demonstrates this.

The very first time we came across leopard Tuli was about a year and a half old – and to my knowledge she had never seen a leopard before. This makes her reaction on this occasion intriguing.

We were walking on a track in a pine plantation, with Tuli approximately ten metres ahead of me when the encounter happened. Suddenly, after stopping and peering down the track, she silently ran back to me and sat behind me – while again peering down the track. Somewhat baffled by her behaviour, I also looked ahead of us and saw a leopard in the centre of the track about 50 metres away.

The leopard was in a compromised position as it was defecating. It then sensed our presence, turned to look in our direction, and in a blur it slipped away.

What intrigued me about Tuli's behaviour was that it seemed that she had instinctively recognised the leopard and the potential danger it posed to her because of what it was, and so she had put me, for protection, between her and the leopard. This illustrates the keen and deeply entrenched instinct of the *Africanis* type of dog. Certainly no one had taught her to react like this. Interestingly (and a little bit odd), Tuli would exhibit exactly the same behaviour whenever a bee entered my cabin. If I was standing, she would always move to sit behind me, placing me between her and the bee. Identical behaviour, but for a vastly different type of potential danger.

In contrast, and very strangely, Tuli did not show this behaviour when encountering a honey badger, possibly the most courageous (and audacious) mammal in Africa.

Once when heading down into leopard gorge – with Tuli on a lead, our usual precaution when venturing down there – a honey badger dashed along an embankment some 50 metres away. Tuli, forgetting or perhaps not even thinking that she was on a lead, lunged forward, and despite being a relatively small dog weighing some 22 kilograms, almost pulled me off my feet.

Moments later I tried not to think about what could have happened if I had not had her on a lead, and I could not understand why, unlike the incident with leopard, her instinct had not warned her about the great threat a honey badger could have posed to her if she had attempted to pursue it.

Many years later I again witnessed Tuli's lack of instinctive fear of the honey badger. This time she was not on a lead and the outcome could have been fatal. We were walking in a relatively open and flat area, when suddenly she flashed ahead of me at high speed. Initially I thought she had seen a Cape grey mongoose, a creature she would not infrequently chase after.

Next I saw a honey badger appear in front of Tuli from behind a mound of earth. It happened so fast, but by this time she and the honey badger were about 70 metres away from me. I yelled at the top of my voice – a yell I usually reserved to deter charging elephant, lion or leopard. The yell startled and distracted the honey badger which instantly fled and, simultaneously, Tuli flew back to where I was standing – appearing to understand that she had been in mortal danger.

Tuli almost stepped on puff adders on several occasions, and probably would have, had I not seen these deadly snakes and pulled her aside just in time. Her failure to sense these snakes was not a result of her instincts not protecting her but because, as has recently been scientifically shown, puff adders have the amazing ability to be virtually odourless.[35] Thus, combined with their visual camouflage, they are almost invisible to dogs and other potential predators – and of course to their prey.

One of these puff adder incidents has an interesting back-story – a dramatic encounter one night between Homex, a Malawian friend of mine (who works on the property where I live), and a leopard. By a strange

35 Research Article. An ambusher's arsenal: chemical crypsis in the puff adder (*Bitis arietans*). Ashadee Kay Miller, Bryan Maritz, Shannon McKay, Xavier Glaudas and Graham J. Alexander. Published 22 December 2015. https://www.researchgate.net/publication/286932995_An_ambusher's_arsenal_Chemical_crypsis_in_the_puff_adder_Bitis_arietans

coincidence, three weeks earlier, quite out of the blue, Homex had asked me, 'Gareth, if I come across a leopard when walking home at night, what should I do?' I told him that the leopards here are shy and being (like puff adders) masters of camouflage, he would probably not ever see one, but if he did encounter one he should not turn and run but should stand his ground – and the leopard would probably just move away.

On the fateful night, as Homex was approaching the property's electric gate (which has a flood light above it) and was feeling in his pocket for his remote to open the gate, a leopard walked out in front of him and sank to the ground. It was barely five metres away from him. To his absolute credit and bravery, Homex managed to heed my advice and stood his ground.

The leopard had cubs and therefore instead of staying hidden or spiriting herself away, she had shown herself. The next few minutes must have been the longest minutes in Homex's life, before the leopard called her cubs, which appeared behind her, and followed her across the road and down the embankment on the other side.

Homex did not use his remote to open the electric gate that night. Incredibly, he cleared the 1.85 metre gate, and fled down the one kilometre driveway to where he lived.

The following morning Homex contacted me and offered to show me where the encounter had taken place at the gate. Tuli and I headed up the long driveway to meet Homex. She was trotting along beside me when suddenly she veered to the right onto a low embankment. It happened in a flash, but at the time it seemed to play out in slow motion.

I saw ahead of Tuli a large (approximately one metre long) puff adder. Just as she was about to scamper unknowingly onto it, I leapt forward, grabbed her by her collar and pulled her away. And that was just one occasion that I managed to prevent her from stepping onto a puff adder... Such encounters leave one feeling as if one's heart is in one's mouth –

much like Homex must have felt the night before.

'It was as though it had been plucked, Gareth. Quills were everywhere!' a friend reported to me one morning after finding where a leopard (very likely the same leopard Homex had encountered) had killed a porcupine. Tuli and I set out to investigate. We found the place easily. Black and white quills were scattered abundantly on a track on the edge of a pine plantation. Tuli sniffed inquisitively, but also with some caution, at the quills.

I followed her as she trailed off the track and moved several metres into the plantation. Casting around, I saw the site of the battle between the porcupine and the leopard. Vegetation had been disturbed and flattened. Typically, when attacked porcupines will back up or go sideways towards whatever is confronting it, and they have been known to severely injure leopard as well as lion.

I turned around to look for Tuli and found her looking curiously at several quills that were protruding from the base of a pine tree; they looked like black and white darts. Seeing how firmly the quills had penetrated the tree's bark was testament to the determined fight the porcupine had put up.

With Tuli cautiously walking behind me, I followed a trail of quills and drag marks where the leopard had pulled the porcupine from the kill site. The trail led to a tangle of thick vegetation in which the leopard might still have been hidden with its kill. Always believing in the adage that 'discretion is the better part of valour', I backed away with Tuli close at my heels.

As mentioned earlier, for some years now I have undertaken mini-expeditions with guests into the forest and fynbos home of the elephants – *The Secret Elephants Forest Experience*. In the space of two weeks in early 2017, not only would I and my guests have an extraordinary encounter with one of the elephants, but Tuli and I were going to encounter curious and very intriguing evidence of an otang.

Tuli had to stay behind in my cabin whenever I did the forest experiences, and she always looked visibly unhappy about this as I packed my rucksack and closed the cabin door, but she would always be delighted when I returned, tired, several hours later, sniffing at the forest smells on my legs (and at the smell of elephant dung on my hands!).

The elephant encounter took place when I was accompanied on the forest experience by three ladies from England. We were walking on a track deep in the northern section of the forest. We had left the vehicle to explore an area where over the past years I have not only come across very fresh signs of the elephants, but have even heard them on several occasions with my forest experience guests. Hearing the Knysna elephants is usually extremely rare, with sightings by SANParks personnel and visitors to the area in recent years averaging at the most perhaps once or twice annually. So it was, and still is, peculiar that on that particular stretch of track, I would from time to time hear elephants. That day I told my guests (as I do with most guests) about this strange phenomenon.

We walked along the track for about a kilometre and a half, with me pointing out active and inactive ancient (north/south) elephant pathways that bisect the east to west forest track. As we walked that morning neither the ladies nor I could ever have imagined that we had walked past an elephant.

This was revealed when we began walking back to the vehicle.

As we headed back east in the direction from which we had come, the extremely loud crack of a branch being pulled down suddenly echoed in the air, some 30 to 40 metres away to the left of where we were walking. The ladies jumped (as I am sure I did), and their eyes bulged. 'What was that, Gareth?' one of the ladies exclaimed. All this happened in a second or two, by which time I was scanning in the direction from which the sound had come.

And then, hardly believing my eyes, I saw it – an elephant. Typically, when sighting a Knysna elephant, due to the patchy forest light I did not at first know which part of the anatomy of the elephant I was looking at. Then I thought I could make it out. It seemed that I was looking at its hindquarters.

'That,' I said to the ladies, 'was an elephant', and I pointed to my left. Unfortunately the ladies were fairly short and a wall of ferns blocked their view. Realising this, I led them a few metres down the track to where I hoped we might find a spot where they could look into the forest, but still their view was obscured.

We went back to where we had first heard the elephant, but when I looked at where I had seen it, the great grey ghost had vanished – as they do – and only streaks of lemon-coloured light streamed into the gap where it had been.

Despite not being able to see the elephant, the encounter was one that the ladies would never forget. It was a wonderful, almost magical, experience for all of us.

Several days later I accompanied another group on a forest experience and while we were paying our conservation fees at the Diepwalle Forest Station, a SANParks colleague took me to one side and asked, 'Gareth, where were you walking when you were here the other day with your guests?' I told him, and enquired why he was asking.

He then told me that on the same day I had been with the English ladies two German tourists had an extraordinary encounter with an elephant on one of the public hiking trails. The tourists, apparently first time visitors to South Africa, had walked around a bend on the hiking trail – and there it stood.

Their shock must have been enormous, and I would not have been surprised if it later resulted in post-traumatic stress disorder (PTSD) – much like the shock experienced by people seeing an otang. It must have been absolutely terrifying for the German tourists to have rounded the bend and seen an elephant standing there – it would have been terrifying for anyone, for that matter.

About ten or so days later, accompanied by Tuli, I came across intriguing and fresh evidence of an otang. That month was a fruitful one, to say the least, for research on both the elephants and the otang.

It was early on a Saturday morning. The clouds were heavy and dark with the promise of impending rain. Despite the weather, I was determined to take Tuli for a walk, even if it was to be short. I had been busy with forest experiences and felt bad that she had been spending more time than usual in the cabin.

We passed through the electric gate (which by then, after Homex's encounter, had a bold sign attached to it stating, 'Beware of Leopard') and set off west up the dirt road.

We had not walked more than one hundred metres when I saw – and Tuli began sniffing at – the extraordinary tracks. The being had walked along the road – and at times had even put its hands on the ground. And as Tuli and I were investigating the fresh and astonishing tracks, the clouds opened and the rain pelted down on us like bullets.

Within moments the foot and handprints had been obliterated. I had not even had time to photograph what had been one of the clearest trackways of an otang that I had ever seen. But there was nothing for Tuli and me to do but to rush back to the gate and down the driveway to the cabin.

After towelling Tuli relatively dry, and changing into dry clothes, I almost pinched myself to be sure that what we had just seen had not been a dream.

My diary notes for that morning record what had happened:

Very strange spoor on the top of the hill on the main road near right turn. Must have been an otang – but very large, and not just feet, but hands as well. Have not seen otang sign like this before. Tuli sniffing at it, very interested. Rain came down hard, so could not photograph!

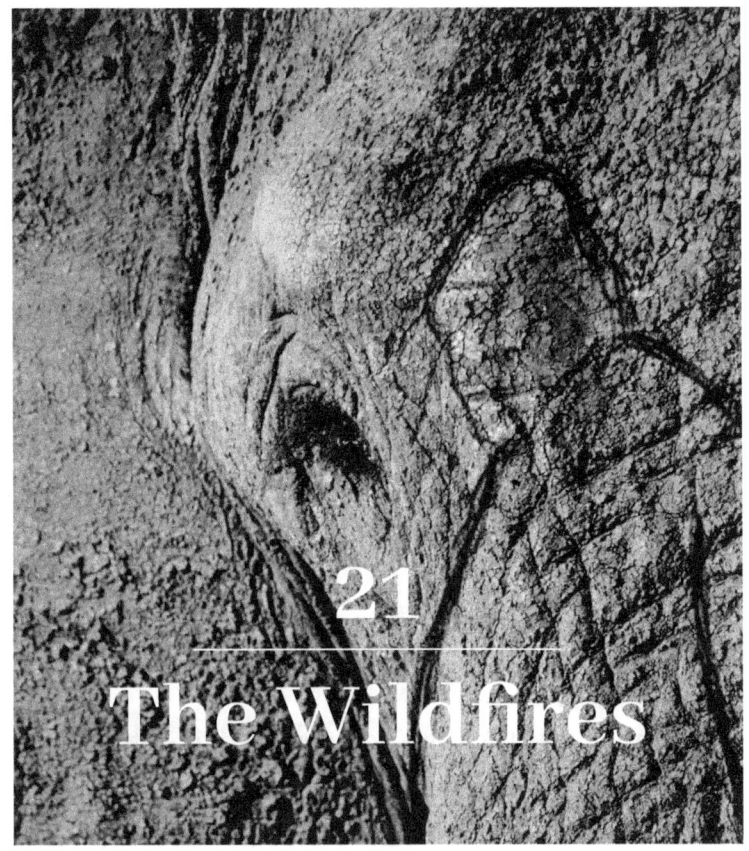

21

The Wildfires

The seventh of June 2017 is a date that is etched into my mind and into the minds of thousands of people who live in the vicinity of the little town of Knysna. It was the date when the inferno struck. Described as the biggest natural disaster in the history of South Africa, wildfires destroyed more than 1 100 homes, burnt to the ground some 20 000 hectares of plantations and fynbos, and resulted in the deaths of nine people and an unknown number of domestic animals. How more people did not die is actually inexplicable. It was almost as if there had been divine intervention.

Two years later the terror of the inferno remains in the psyche of all who witnessed it, and all who survived it. Today, we survivors see smoke where there is no smoke, see blooms of fire at night where there is only darkness, and we shudder whenever we hear the 'whap, whap' of helicopter blades, or the drone of airplanes, all of which instantly take us back to the long days of the firefighting helicopter water bombers overhead and the fire spotter planes.

The day before the inferno the weather forecast predicted that an enormous storm would land on the shores of the southern Cape coast, bringing much needed rain. Living in crippling drought conditions, the inhabitants of this beautiful area grew excited, 'rain at last', we thought – never imagining what the storm's gale force winds would actually bring, turning the place where we live into a burnt and battered war zone.

The gale force wind hit us late in the night. My wooden cabin literally rocked and swayed, and I feared that the west facing windows would burst inwards. An old sheet that I use instead of curtains flapped as wind hissed through the closed but not completely tight-fitting windows. On her couch Tuli turned repeatedly to look in my direction – and equally repeatedly I attempted to say soothing words to her.

Then I saw it. Three kilometres to the south, below where I live on the edge of the forest, a Knysna suburb was igniting. From my kitchen window I saw balls of flame and heard rattling booms. Gas bottles at people's homes were exploding like bombs. The 120 kilometre per hour wind, we learnt later, ignited houses, trees and everything else some 300 metres ahead of the frontlines of the blaze.

On the neighbouring property 500 metres away, I could see and hear vehicles being driven away as the occupants of the twelve wooden houses rapidly evacuated. I then heard vehicles leaving rapidly from the place where I live. My phone rang. It was my landlord telling me that the authorities recommended that we all evacuate and move into the town.

After speaking to my landlord, I thought of the chaos that must be happening in the town as it became encircled by crazy wildfire. Though I did not know it at the time, hundreds of townsfolk were pouring onto Thesen's Island in the Knysna lagoon trying to escape the inferno. 'Perhaps,' I thought to myself, 'it would be better to stay here.' The last 'Great Fire' was in 1869, and back then the indigenous forest did not burn, apart from the edges. Because of the topography and the prevailing wind, the fire skirted the central forest. I knew that between me and the approaching inferno was a broad swath of indigenous forest – and this could mean I would be protected.

I heard a hammering at my door. It was my neighbour Arnaud. He came inside and we rapidly discussed the situation – and my theory that the indigenous forest could protect us. He agreed with me, and said that his partner Barbara-Ann (and their two dogs), as well as two other neighbours, would also be staying. We agreed that what was going on down below us in town, with the mass evacuations, must be mayhem and a nightmare.

And so the long days of vigil on the farm began – days that blurred into one another, so much so that today none of us can really comprehend the sequence of events.

The swath of indigenous forest did save us that night, but the following morning the inferno swept around it and headed rapidly in our direction.

At one stage twenty-six different wildfires were burning simultaneously. The ingredients of the inferno were the combination of extreme drought conditions, the hundreds of thousands of alien trees (which, unlike indigenous species, burn extremely hot) and the howling gale force wind – a lethal concoction that produced the perfect fire storm.

Within a day or so the fire had stretched more than 300 kilometres up along the southern Cape coast and at one point was spreading at the rate of one kilometre a minute. At one stage both ends of the road, both into and out of Knysna, were closed because of the inferno and the town and its inhabitants were virtually encircled by raging flames.

Through a combination of the extraordinary efforts of the firefighters and, I suspect, a miracle, the place where I live and the two bordering properties were not engulfed, though on numerous occasions over the next two weeks we very nearly did burn down as a result of flare-ups. The fire came within 150 metres of our cabins. We barely slept at night, and when we did, it was for short intervals with someone on watch at almost all times.

The three properties and the nearby township were the only areas in some 120 square kilometres that did not burn. From the air we were a tiny circular island of relative green in a sea of grey, with the downside being that we were the only area that could still burn. And so we lived on our nerves, never knowing when it would be – almost inevitably, it seemed at times – our turn to burn.

The local firefighters, as well as their colleagues flown in from elsewhere in South Africa and internationally, worked tirelessly. In total some 1 200 firefighters; 350 vehicles, four SANDF Oryx helicopters, four Huey helicopters, two fixed winged bomber planes and two spotter planes had been deployed. It was the largest mobilisation of its kind in the history of South Africa.

Because we were very close to the local township, every effort was made to ensure that we did not burn. If we went, and the fire swept into the township and the informal settlements, the toll would have been unimaginable – horrendous. As it was, nine people were tragically killed, two of whom were firefighters.

After several days, with fires still flaring up periodically, we made the wrong decision to risk driving into town to replenish supplies. This could potentially have been a fatal mistake.

Arnaud stayed behind to work with the firefighters while I accompanied Barbara-Ann (who drove) and our mutual neighbour Martin (plus Tuli and Barbara-Ann and Arnaud's two dogs). The decision to make the trip was almost immediately regretted. We had travelled only a kilometre when we came across a truck parked in the middle of the road, in front of which was a fallen tree. Men with chainsaws were desperately cutting up the tree to clear the road. The heat was intense. Both sides of the road were like a gigantic braai (barbecue) pit, with searing hot coals of smouldering logs. It felt as if we were trapped inside an immense oven. Car tyres are known to burst in such conditions, and I began to worry about the car's fuel tank. Thankfully, the tree was cleared and we continued onwards.

A kilometre further on visibility was virtually reduced to zero as powerful gusts of wind-swirled smoke surrounded us. I spoke to Barbara-Ann in my calmest of tones to allay her alarm, telling her to put the headlights on and to drive more slowly. Thankfully the waves of chokingly thick smoke cleared and we emerged, blinking, into almost clear air at a point where the dirt road joins the tarred road. The dogs behaved exceptionally throughout the disaster, remaining calm and trusting in spite of the drama.

We descended the long hill towards the town. Like a veil lifting, the clearer air revealed the horror of the extent of the wildfires. As we approached the outskirts of the town we began to see the burnt-out houses. We were shocked. Places and dwellings once familiar to us were now gutted, blackened, roofless ruins. People's homes were just scabby shells; everything had been lost.

As we drove into the town we continued to see the dismal sights of destruction. Incredibly, moving like fiery giant tumbleweeds, balls of the inferno had burst into one house then seemingly bounced over a neighbouring home, leaving it relatively unscathed, only to crash into another and destroy it. It looked as if the residential areas on the very edge of the town had been left in the wake of a fierce military battle.

In town we parked at the Methodist church where Arnaud and Barbara-Ann worked as volunteer social workers. As we got out of the car, we saw and heard to our horror that there in the centre of the town a hillside less than 400 metres away was on fire. Soon the crackling and popping sounds of the fire were drowned out by the deep 'whapping' of a helicopter as it water-bombed the flames. By deciding to go into town we had literally gone out of the frying pan into the fire.

After collecting supplies and bottled water we drove out of town. We wanted to be home, and prayed we would make it. Mercifully the return journey, though at times somewhat arduous, was less frightening than the one we had endured earlier that morning.

Whether it was that night, or another night – the days became blurred and we lost track of time – a surreal incident took place, one that illustrated the callous and exploitative nature of some people's dark hearts in a time of a disaster. By this time we had had very little sleep for a number of days. Despite the fires still being visible on the outskirts of the farm, we thought that night we should be able to get a few hours' sleep.

With Tuli settled on her couch, I lay down on my bed. I was exhausted and fell asleep almost immediately.

But just minutes later I was abruptly woken by the loud hammering of hands on the windows and the sides of the cabin. Voices shouted, 'Paramedics! Evacuate!' I drew back the curtain and was almost blinded by men wearing head torches. As my eyes adjusted, I saw a large woman in ordinary clothing standing in front of the men, and then saw that the men were wearing what seemed to be – and soon proved to be – fake uniforms.

'We are paramedics', the woman shouted, 'and we must take your blood pressure.' What I was seeing and hearing was completely surreal. Intuition and plain common sense screamed at me that everything was completely wrong. Despite this, I grabbed my evacuation 'jump bag' (a bag containing valuables, wallet, ID, passport, and small personal items), put Tuli on her lead, opened the cabin door and stepped outside.

'We must take your blood pressure,' said the woman, 'and then you must come with us.' She pointed at two vehicles which could only be described as old farm trucks. 'We must take your neighbours with us too,' she emphasised.

'No, no, no,' I thought to myself, 'this is not right.' Then one of the men attempted to grab my jump bag. I shrugged him away, and walked briskly with Tuli to Arnaud and Barbara-Ann's cabin. They were awake and in a few sentences I briefed them on the situation and on what I thought – basically that a scam was going on. Then there was a loud eruption of fire nearby. These flare-ups are almost like the burst of a flamethrower – sudden, abrupt and very scary. I turned and saw the woman and the men fleeing in panic for the trucks, and once inside they roared away with wheels spinning, never to be seen again. Their departure was almost comical.

A few days later, when the fires had calmed down somewhat, a mobile clinic arrived at our cabins and neatly uniformed paramedics emerged from the vehicle. They were very pleasant and kind. They had come to see how we were and to check our blood pressure now that the major stage of the disaster had passed.

The gang from a few nights before had been scam artists, bogus paramedics, wanting the possessions in our jump bags. A not dissimilar scam, we heard later, was operating in the townships. Trucks would appear late in the night and bleary-eyed occupants of houses were told, 'We have been seconded by the municipality to save your possessions and furniture. Please help us to put them all in the back of the truck.'

It was an extraordinary time – but as with all times of high drama, there were also some moments of dark humour. One night when there was yet another flare-up close to the cabins, a neighbour who had also decided to stay on the farm leapt into his pick-up truck to escape the advancing flames and reversed at high speed – directly towards my cabin. Arnaud and I yelled at him to stop. He came to an abrupt halt just a few feet from the rear wooden wall of the cabin. 'Shoo,' I said to Arnaud, 'he almost knocked my cabin down before it burnt down.'

A friend of mine, Dom (not to be confused with Domi Diane), lives in a blue house on his property adjoining the place where I live. Dom, who lives on his own, had been plagued for days and days with flare-ups on his land – and whenever we met it was clear that his nerves, like ours, were badly frayed (but perhaps a little more so in his case).

It became a ritual of mine to check out of my office window every evening to make sure there were no more flare-ups at Dom's place.

One evening while I was checking I saw that yet another flare-up had erupted and it was dangerously close to Dom's blue house. I quickly called him on my phone, saying as he answered, 'Dom, are you at home?' But before I could even finish the sentence he said in a rush, 'I know! I am on f..king fire again, and I cannot get any f..king joy out of the f..king fire brigade!' Thankfully the firefighters arrived in a truck minutes later and in a series of efficient manoeuvres (watched by Arnaud and myself from the rise above the cabins), they incredibly managed to save Dom's blue house from being burnt to the ground.

The bravery of the firefighters throughout the entire disaster never ceased to amaze us. On another occasion, neighbours of Dom's were fleeing from the fires in their luxury Jeep. There were flames on both sides of the track they were driving down and the car's air filter caught alight. As they were approaching our gate, a firefighter appeared seemingly from nowhere, told them to release the bonnet, shoved his hands into the engine, ripped out the burning air filter, and threw it onto the side of the track. Dom's neighbours then proceeded with their evacuation down to the town.

We had no electricity for a number of days. I had noticed that a transformer box on the power lines across the farm had been smouldering. Eventually, almost forlornly, it fell to the ground. One morning a municipal electrician and his team drove past our cabins in a big truck with a crane on it. We grew excited. Perhaps we were about to have electricity again. And in a few hours we did.

As the electrician and his team left, I went to the road to thank them. The burly Afrikaans-speaking electrician smiled and said, pointing to the old burnt-out transformer in the back of the truck, '*No probs, Meneer, daar was 'n gat in die doos*' (No problem, Sir, there was a hole in the box).

There was a diversity of wild creatures living with us on the farm, amongst them flocks of guineafowls, a troop of vervet monkeys, a family of francolin and from time to time, of course, Homex's leopard. I was worried about them during the worst of the wildfires.

To my amazement, a few days after the main fires struck, on a morning when the smoke was lifting, the guineafowls appeared and came to visit us, as did the monkeys and the francolins.

They had all made it unscathed.

With the electricity restored, I was able for the first time in days to check my emails and Facebook. I received numerous emails and messages from people both nationally and internationally who were concerned about how the Knysna elephants had been affected by the wildfires. People had naturally assumed that the entire Knysna forest had been devastated by the fire. But the elephants were fine. When the smoke from the first fires had cleared, I walked with Tuli to the gate from which there is a wonderful view that encompasses the majority of the central Knysna forests and the hundreds of square kilometres of mountain fynbos beyond them.

As I scanned the area with binoculars I could see that the majority of the elephants' range had been untouched by the mainly coastal fires. As mentioned previously, due to the topography of the land and the prevailing wind, the central Knysna forests (apart from the edges) did not burn during the Great Fire of 1869, and nor did the central forests burn during the 2017 wildfires. But I delayed replying to the heartfelt enquiries. Although the elephants are as important as people, I felt it would be inappropriate and insensitive at that early stage to respond to enquiries about the elephants when there was still such a great humanitarian crisis unfolding.

As the days passed and things became relatively calm, Tuli and I ventured out into the scorched land to investigate the toll the wildfires had had on the local wildlife. After covering a considerable area, to my amazement and immense joy, I discovered not a single fatality. Of course, I am not saying that there were no losses, only that after extensive searches

I found none. It was heartening and remarkable. It highlighted the fact that the animals, living within a totally unfenced, free-ranging area, had reacted ahead of the advancing fire and had successfully sought safety. Likewise, I trusted that the otangs had also reacted in the way the other wild creatures had done. In the following days Tuli and I increasingly found on the now cooled burnt ground the footprints of bushbuck, baboon, bushpig, vervet monkey, mongoose, honey badger and porcupine. They were continuing to go about their lives, living in the now.

One morning I took a photograph of a forest buzzard with the moon in the background, as it launched itself from a stark and lonely tree protruding singly on the otherwise almost lunar landscape. The raptor, to me at least, represented the proverbial phoenix rising from the ashes.

22
Solitary Grey Ghosts

At 11:25 am on 16 November 2017, completely out of the blue, I received an email headed 'Hello my friend' from Liz, my SANParks Knysna elephant researcher friend:

Hi Gareth

How are you doing?

Are you at home?

Can I come and see you?

Warm regards

Liz

Apart from chance meetings in town, I had had no real contact with Liz for almost three years, which in a sense was a little strange as we had been good friends. Circumstances, of which none were negative, had simply resulted in our drifting apart. Therefore her email asking to see me at incredibly short notice was very much of a surprise. I certainly did not have to navel-gaze to understand that something was afoot.

I replied to Liz: 'Nice surprise! Sure Liz. What time?' to which she suggested in four hours' time, at 3:30 pm.

Liz and I first met back in 2008 when she, an elephant biologist, moved from the Tembe Elephant Park in KwaZulu-Natal to work for SANParks in the Garden Route National Park. Unsurprisingly, with elephants in common, and liking each other, we became firm friends. 'You were my first Knysna friend,' Liz once said to me. Also, more by coincidence than deliberate planning, Liz became my neighbour for a while when she moved into a cabin next to mine at Blaricum Heights Farm.

With her elephant background, when she started work with SANParks she had been very excited by the publication of Lori Eggert's and my peer-reviewed 2007 paper announcing the results of our DNA census study (which identified five females – and in the follow-up 2009 study a sixth female that we had missed the first time around. This excluded fieldwork evidence of three bulls and a few calves).

Very soon, though, Liz became perplexed. Despite the DNA and field proof, certain SANParks colleagues told her adamantly that I was wrong, that only one Knysna elephant existed, and that the Knysna elephants were a 'functionally extinct population'. It was a very difficult time for her in her workplace and put emotional pressure on her. 'They do not even like me talking to you,' she once said. She was living next door to a friend who knew that a small, but viable, elephant population existed, but daily had to contend with the darkly negative rhetoric that the elephants were 'finished'. In later years one of her superiors even said to her, 'This last elephant must just *vrek* (die) now and that will be the end of all this.' I once told her that she was being bullied in her workplace. Liz, a fiercely resolute person, replied, 'Bullied? No. Ill-treated. Yes.'

In 2012 Liz took over the SANParks Knysna elephants monitoring project and quickly restructured how the monitoring should be undertaken. SANParks' previous way of monitoring the elephants was to have Wilfred and Karel track them whenever the opportunity arose – and for them to attempt to photograph them. This was an invasive method, creating stress for the elephants since they were effectively being routinely hunted. It was also a stressful and potentially dangerous method for Wilfred and Karel in the dense field conditions where visibility was extremely low. The fact that neither of the men had been killed over the years of monitoring is due entirely to the forgiving disposition of the elephants – and the fact that the elephants knew them.

When she took over the monitoring project Liz halted the 'hunt and photograph' monitoring method and trained the forest guards to measure the circumference of dung bolus to determine age and, in turn, attempt to identify individuals. Somewhat strangely, though, in a 2019 article she stated:

> By 2014 we had dung measurements spanning two years, which ruled out mature males and calves, and a limited number of photographs that suggested one female ...

(For purposes of identification and clarity, I will later refer to this female as 'Liz's elephant' or 'her elephant'.)

This was most odd as during my 2009 DNA census project several of the fifty measured samples indicated quite young elephants, including one tiny sample collected by Wilfred and Karel with my filmmaker friend Mark van Wijk during the filming of our documentary, *The Search for the Knysna Elephants* (part of the filming took place during the second DNA project). In the documentary one sees Karel examining the tiny elephant dropping and saying to Wilfred that the dropping was *'n bietjie klein* (a bit small) which was a modest understatement as the dropping indicated a calf of approximately only three years old. In addition, several of the other measured DNA samples were large and could have been from adult bulls.

An aspect of the Knysna elephants that Liz had a problem fathoming was that they do not move in herds, but usually singly or as a mother with a calf. She came from a background of typical savannah elephant social structures (herds) and, apart from single bulls, finding tracks of a single elephant was an anomaly to Liz. I too had come from a background of typical elephant social structures, and finding signs of single elephants in the forest and fynbos had also initially seemed strange to me, but in time I developed a hypothesis as to why the elephants usually move singly – and it centred on predation, or rather the lack of predation. Lion have not existed in the Knysna area for more than two hundred years.

Knysna elephants are savannah elephants, but are occasionally erroneously termed 'forest elephants' by the media. The forest elephant is a separate species, the smallest of the three elephant species, which exists in the dense forests of West and Central Africa. Unlike the savannah elephant, for reasons that are not completely understood, they are generally solitary in nature, with groupings made up of a female and her dependant offspring, similar to the evidence I was seeing with the Knysna elephants. It seems that, unlike savannah elephants, young female forest elephants disperse from their mothers (as young bull savannah elephants do, while the young females remain within their kin group) when reaching sexual maturity – hence keeping the forest elephant grouping always small. It is theorised that forest elephants are more solitary due to the absence of lion and hyena in the dense forest habitat, and therefore do not have to move in 'safety in numbers' groupings as savannah elephants do.

Soon after beginning my research on the Knysna elephants, their largely solitary nature became apparent. Occasionally I would find signs of a mother and calf moving together (and I had also had the good fortune to have the sightings of a mother and calf on two occasions). Equally occasionally I would find signs of three elephants moving together made up, I presumed from the very different size of the footprints of a bull, an adult cow and a large calf. In the early years of my study, I not uncommonly came across the tracks of the distinctive foot-printed Strangefoot accompanied by The Youngster – and I very briefly caught a glimpse of them together at The Secret Place. From the measurement of the hind foot diameter, I estimated that at the time Strangefoot was fourteen years old, and The Youngster approximately eight years old – thus, interestingly, not a mother and calf grouping. As time passed it became clear that this intriguing pairing had dissolved at some point, and I repeatedly found that Strangefoot was moving singly.

White settlers had eradicated lions from the Knysna area by 1775. My theory (and I could well be wrong) was that because, like the forest elephants, the Knysna elephants can safely move singly because of the lack of natural predators. And yet at the same time, through vocal and olfactory communication, they can still maintain contact with other members of the population – elephant infrasound can travel for distances of up to ten kilometres or more. When in the forest with Lyall Watson and discussing how through infrasound and the sense of smell the Knysna elephants are constantly communicating with one another, Lyall said with a smile, 'It is like elephant email, Gareth!'

The non-existence of natural predators also seems to be reflected in the Knysna elephants' sleeping habits. Without the fear of an attack by a lion pride, they seem to feel confident and comfortable enough to lie down to sleep, despite being alone. From time to time I would find places where an elephant had lain down to sleep in the mountain fynbos country. (Remember too the story of Wilfred and Karel encountering a sleeping elephant.) Normally adult savannah elephants very rarely lie down. This is behaviour reserved only for calves who, when sleeping, will be protectively encircled by standing adults.

Unfortunately for the Knysna elephants there could be a negative aspect to their solitary behaviour and that is a potentially higher than normal rate of calf mortality. Allomothering, in general terms, is the care of infants by those in a family group, other than just the mother. Apart from enabling protection and guidance, elephant allomothering allows young female elephants who have not yet calved to learn how to raise babies. I have a theory that lack of allomothering experience (particularly in first-time mothers), could have resulted in higher calf mortality with Knysna elephants over the decades, and this is reflected in the population's almost static growth rate.

Local records certainly suggest high Knysna calf mortality. Between 1922 and 1925 several dead calves were found, as were three others between 1937 and 1939. Dead calves were also found in 1942 and 1968. Given the immense range of the elephants, combined with the dense vegetation, whether forest or mountain fynbos, it is surprising that any dead calves were found at all. As mentioned earlier, a helicopter crashed in the forest in 1999, and despite extensive ground and air searches it was only found by accident in 2006. This illustrates the low probability of finding dead elephant calves – and therefore suggests that those that were found represent a very minimal figure of those that have actually died over the years. In 1980[36] it was suggested that there was possibly a 60 to 80 per cent mortality of young Knysna calves – compared with a 7.5 per cent mortality in the Addo Elephant National Park.

In 1970, Nick Carter concluded in his Knysna elephant survey that eleven Knysna elephants existed. Some forty years later, combining our DNA population results, and evidence gleaned from my fieldwork, my estimation of the number of Knysna elephants was remarkably (and worryingly) similar to Nick's estimation (and very similar to an estimation dating back to 1914 – that of twelve elephants).

It is a perplexing and worrying situation.

36 Hall-Martin A. (1980). Elephant survivors. *Oryx*, 15: 355-362.
https://doi.org/10.1017/S0030605300028830

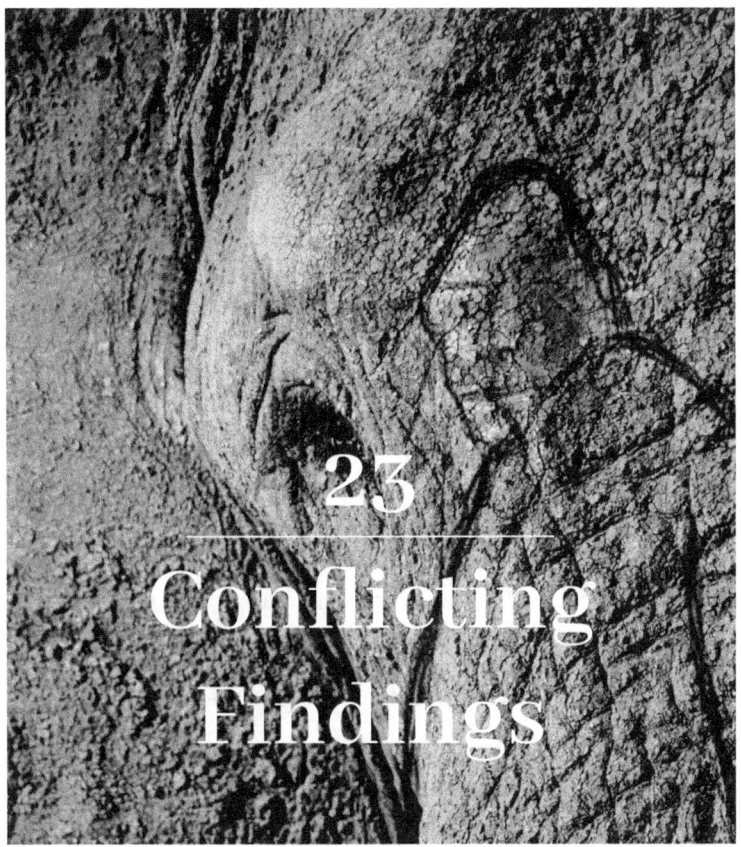

23
Conflicting Findings

In 2016 Liz established a trail camera survey to attempt to learn more about the numbers, ages and behaviour of the Knysna elephants. She set up forty camera stations and the project ran for fifteen months.

It was the (then unpublished) results of this camera survey that Liz, at very short notice, had come to see me about on the afternoon of 16 November 2017.

She arrived with her laptop on which she wanted to show me images and video footage from her camera survey. In short, she told me that over the duration of the survey she had captured images of the same elephant (Liz's elephant) one hundred and forty times, and no images of any other elephants.

'What do you think has happened to the others?' Liz asked me. 'Do you think it could be disease?' To me it was almost preposterous to think, as she seemed to be suggesting, that this elephant was the very last Knysna elephant.

During the same time period as the camera survey I had been regularly conducting my *Secret Elephants Forest Experience* with guests and I had repeatedly come across evidence of other elephants, and elephants of different ages. I told Liz this.

The results of her survey did not concern me too much, but they certainly had me puzzled. Inwardly I felt there must be an explanation for her results; for example, perhaps the trail camera methodology was not an appropriate one (and therefore an inaccurate one) for determining elephant numbers in their undulating dense forest and fynbos habitat. I felt that if this methodology was used it should be done in conjunction with other methods of census – or at least in conjunction with the tried, tested and accepted faecal DNA methodology, which would provide a comparison for the reliability of the camera survey. If dual methods had been undertaken, greater accuracy would have resulted.

Thoughts went through my mind that late afternoon such as, 'Had placement of the cameras biased her results?' 'Has Liz misidentified elephants captured by the cameras, and she has mistakenly concluded the images were all of "her" elephant?' 'Had she established the camera stations in places that were a true representation of the entire range of the Knysna elephants, or just a portion of their vast range?'

In an attempt to test the camera survey results, I asked Liz to check the location of 'her' elephant on 1 February 2017 on her laptop. That was the day when, with three guests, I had a brief sighting of an elephant. Liz checked her records and then named a very different locality in an area far from where I had had my sighting. 'Yes,' she quietly conceded. 'What you saw must have been another elephant then.'

As the afternoon turned to evening, Liz told me about 'her' elephant. It was clear that she had grown emotionally attached to her and was concerned that she was not accompanied by a calf. Later, for almost half an hour, Liz showed me some camera trap video and still images of 'her' elephant on her laptop. When I saw these I recognised the characteristics of one particular Knysna elephant that I knew of. This female elephant is physically strangely bull-like, robustly built, with a sloping underbelly (a male characteristic), has a distinctly wrinkled forehead and, somewhat strangely for her mature adult age (approximately forty-five years old), relatively underdeveloped breasts – indicating that she might not ever have had a calf or had not had a calf for many years.

Seeing the images and video of this elephant I was convinced that she was the very same elephant captured in a series of remarkable photographs taken over a decade before by Hylton Herd, formerly of SANParks. One of the photographs was featured in *The Secret Elephants*.

As with Liz's current images, back in 2008 this elephant was photographed with no accompanying calf.

In *The Secret Elephants*, I had written of this elephant:

> But it was upon seeing these photographs that I became perplexed. Normally it is not difficult to determine the sex of male and female elephants, but this elephant seemed to have a combination of male and female characteristics. The head was angular when viewed from the side (unlike the more rounded shape of males), indicating a female. Yet I could see in some of the photographs that the elephant's underbelly was slanted at an angle, a characteristic of males. All I could be really certain of

was that the elephant appeared to be middle aged and was in fine, if not robust condition.

I pondered over the photographs for hours but could not come to a definite conclusion about this elephant's sex. Though I felt the elephant was most likely a female, I could not be one hundred per cent certain. It was at that point that I forwarded the photos to Joyce Poole (my respected elephant expert colleague). I think Joyce was as confounded as I was. She also felt that the elephant had both male and female characteristics, and therefore could not say with any certainty what the sex was. She agreed that the elephant was middle aged, and in very good condition. In my research records the elephant is referred to rather clinically as 'middle aged – sex unknown'. This elephant is yet another part of the mystery of the world's most southerly elephants.

That evening I told Liz that I felt it was likely that the elephant photographed in 2008 and 'her' elephant was the same elephant. I went on to tell her that I suspected that the elephant could (sadly and unfortunately) be barren, unable to have calves, which explained why back in 2008, and now, a decade later, she has never been photographed accompanied by a calf. Under optimum conditions, calving intervals are usually every four years, and in the past decade this elephant, if fertile, could have given birth to two calves. Her barren state would also explain her underdeveloped breasts (as well as, hypothetically, her strangely bull-like physical characteristics). I knew at the time that at least two bulls existed within the Knysna elephant population – potential mates for Liz's elephant. Footprint size is the giveaway when determining the sex of adult elephants. At the age of twenty-five the diameter of a bull's spoor is already larger than that of an adult female. For the past three years the larger of the two bulls had consistently come into musth (his musth period always beginning in October/November each year and tapering off in April/May), and I had found signs of him accompanying females each year (once with an adult female, and twice with a young but sexually mature female) for a period of a week which is the approximate time a bull remains with a female as he 'guards' her from other bulls during the mating period.

So it was clear to me that at least one breeding bull had been active for the past three years.

The trail camera footage Liz showed me that evening was intriguing. 'Her' elephant would repeatedly touch the cameras with her trunk, and even lie down in front of cameras. Only Liz and her colleague Mel 'serviced' the cameras, and I began to think this elephant had become familiar with Liz and Mel via their scent repeatedly being left on the cameras – as the Knysna elephants clearly knew Wilfred, Karel and me by our scent (more about this a little later).

After viewing the footage Liz told me that an orphaned male calf was presently being cared for in the Addo Elephant National Park (some 300 kilometres from Knysna) and that she was proposing that it be moved to the Garden Route National Park to be introduced to 'her' elephant. 'It is not a conservation project,' Liz said to me, 'but an act of animal welfare to help a lonely elephant, and for her to pass on her knowledge.'

Though knowing that Liz's elephant was not the last Knysna elephant, initially I felt that if the elephant was barren, there might be some merit in her plan – but that evening I was reacting with my heart and not with my head.

Over the next few days my opinion of bringing the orphaned calf to the area changed. Instead of reacting with my heart, I became pragmatic. Clearly the calf should ideally be integrated into a family herd in the land of its birth. Should Liz's elephant not adopt him, he would be wandering here in a totally foreign environment to the land of his birth since the Garden Route National Park and Addo are contrasting habitats. He would be wandering here with no knowledge of the land and no knowledge of the food plants.

Instead of a well-intentioned animal welfare project, bringing the orphan to Knysna would potentially be a move that would create stress and trauma for the orphan, and I expressed this view to Liz. Thankfully her proposed plan did not materialise – and in the months ahead the orphan was successfully integrated into a family herd at Addo.

Three weeks after our meeting in November, Liz and I got together again and she told me a curious story about an encounter with 'her' elephant – a story that convinced me that the elephant had indeed become very familiar with her and Mel.

The year before Mel and Liz were driving in a fynbos area on the edge of the forest looking for a good location for the placement of a camera station. As they turned a corner, they suddenly saw the elephant on the track, approximately 80 metres away.

Mel immediately switched off the engine and, in complete awe, the two women watched the elephant. Liz told me how she had been amazed that the elephant had just stood there and had not moved away. It was an unprecedented sighting of a Knysna elephant from a vehicle. Liz and Mel watched her for about fifteen minutes before the elephant slowly turned, moved off the track and disappeared into the tall fynbos.

After the elephant had moved out of sight, Liz and Mel got out of the vehicle. Close to where the elephant had been standing was a pile of droppings, and they wished (as a part of their research project) to measure bolus circumference. They walked up to the dung pile.

With her back to the place where the elephant had moved off the track, Liz bent down to pick up a ball of dung. Mel was standing opposite Liz, and was facing her. As Liz bent down she heard Mel say in a low voice, 'Liz, the elephant is behind you.' Liz turned and there, no more than four metres away in the dense fynbos, stood the elephant.

Both women hastily retreated to their vehicle.

It was an extraordinary encounter, and one that I would have never believed if it had not been Liz herself telling me about it. The fact that one of these notoriously shy and elusive elephants had remained on the track on the approach of the vehicle (remembering that it would have heard the vehicle from some distance away) was extraordinary enough. But for the elephant to have allowed the women to approach within a few metres of her, on foot, is almost unbelievable.

Clearly the elephant knows Liz and Mel – and clearly knows too that they pose no threat to her.

After hearing the story I said to Liz, 'Through your scent left on the trail cameras after you and Mel have serviced them numerous times, I think this curious elephant has become habituated to you both. And,' I continued, 'it can very likely distinguish between the sound of your vehicle and other vehicles. If a very real familiarisation had not existed, you, and perhaps both of you, would have been killed that day. She knows you, Liz.'

I then told Liz of some of the not dissimilar experiences Wilfred, Karel and I had had over the years with the elephants – clearly they knew us too from our scent. Liz knew of many of these experiences but I retold several of them as they emphasised the familiarisation between this particular elephant and her and Mel.

I told her how for months, when walking to the Secret Place, I would place small rocks on the boughs of a tree that lay across the track, and how an elephant, or elephants, would remove them and put them on the ground and how, in turn, the next time I was passing by, I would replace the rocks. And so it went on. The rocks were our calling cards.

I told Liz about the occasion an elephant had sought me out by following my footprints by scent. I also reminded her of the encounter when Wilfred and Karel had almost walked into a sleeping elephant, and how after it woke up it walked up to where Wilfred was crouching behind a yellowwood tree – and had practically stood over him – before calmly moving away.

These encounters took place only because the elephants know a few of us. And, I must emphasise, they know us far better than we know them because of their remarkable sense of smell – and their remarkable intelligence.

I then told Liz of a fascinating encounter I had had just months before. It was an incident she had not heard before. I was with two guests on one of my *Secret Elephants Forest Experiences* when the encounter took place.

Though I did not know it when I first met the guests (a husband and wife), they were Knysna elephant denialists who believed that the stories of the elephants' existence were being maintained for tourism purposes.

A couple of hours into the forest experience, during which I had shown them droppings, footprints and feeding signs of the elephants, the couple, who were very nice people, admitted to me that they had previously been disbelievers in the elephants and that now they realised that they were obviously very wrong in their assumption. We had a chuckle about this and then proceeded with the forest experience, never imagining that one of the elephants was about to proclaim their kind's existence!

I walked the guests up to three active elephant pathways. It is a place that is special to me – and to the elephants. The pathway leads into an enchanted and very peaceful glade. Here the elephants would pause and linger for a while before continuing north on the pathway. To me at least, the peaceful glade was of special importance to the elephants. Whenever I go there, I can feel the peaceful aura of the place, and everybody I take to the edge of the glade feels it too. Respecting its specialness, I never enter the glade.

I had taken a few steps onto one of the pathways with the guests just behind me when I heard the lady say in a hushed but alarmed tone, 'What is that, Gareth?' I turned, and saw that she was pointing to our left. 'I think I heard branches breaking.'

We stopped and listened and indeed there was a rustling sound some 40 metres away. We continued listening when, to our astonishment, all three of us clearly heard the low rumbling vocalisation of an elephant. This was incredible. Instead of staying silent and motionless, the elephant had passively and without aggression advertised its presence and close proximity to us.

Though not totally believing I would receive a response, I imitated a low greeting rumble back to the elephant. To our further astonishment, the elephant replied – to which I again responded and in turn received a further reply.

Liz left that night in November 2017 no doubt pondering on what I had told her that evening of the Knysna elephants' familiarisation with those of us who have spent protracted periods of time in their footsteps, and in close proximity to them.

Though she did not say so, I think she had already known that 'her' elephant was familiar with her and Mel.

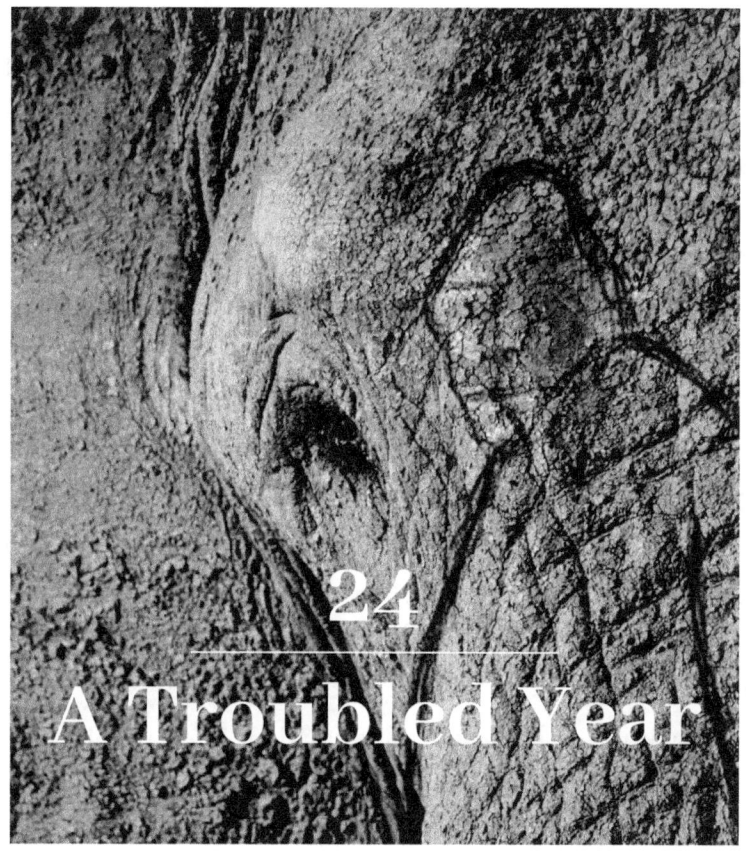

24
A Troubled Year

The following year, 2018, was one much associated with death – and towards the end it almost culminated in my own demise.

The year began in an ominous way with an encounter that was like an indication of what was to follow in the months ahead.

On the morning of 2 January Tuli (who at nine years old was showing signs of deafness) and I were searching for signs, particularly footprints, of otang. We had been doing these patrols consistently for many months. In my rucksack I had a tape measure for measuring tracks, a note pad for recording findings, a GPS, plaster of Paris to make a cast of tracks, and a camera to photograph findings. And I always carried a stout stick.

A few days before while walking back to the cabin, Tuli and I had become very aware of the smell of carrion. As we were returning home on 2 January, and close to the place where we had detected the pungent smell, my bush instincts suddenly and urgently alerted me to danger. I spun around, yelled loudly, and raised my stout stick. A large dog skidded to a stop just a metre away, before turning and speeding off. This all happened in an instant. The dog had been running quietly and stealthily and was clearly intent on attacking Tuli.

It certainly was not a case of a friendly dog with a lolling tongue, loping up to say 'hello'. This dog had a deadly intent. It was a rough, heavily muscled pit-bull cross type of dog with cropped ears. I bent down to calm Tuli. I had never seen her so scared and shocked before – and Tuli did not scare easily. The fact that she had not heard the approach of the would-be attacker was a further indication that her deafness was advancing.

Safely back in the cabin after the incident I felt perplexed. Where I live in the Western Cape there is a low incidence of rabies, so this did not explain the dog's extreme behaviour. I then realised that it could be an escaped fight-dog, used in that appalling 'sport'. This explained the dog's cropped ears. The owners crop the ears to limit the areas that opponent dogs can seize during a fight. I remembered the tragic case the year before of an old lady who had been collecting wood when she was attacked by a dog and died as a result its savage bites. Fearing the risk Tuli's attacker posed to other dogs, as well as to people and particularly children, I reported the incident to the local animal welfare society and notified people living in my area.

The following day I went out to the place of the rank smell and found its source. A dead dog.

After the incident I had noticed that Tuli was slowing down. Initially I thought that this was a coincidence. Little did I know that serious matters were afoot. She still continued to enjoy long otang patrols with me and as usual would dart away at speed whenever the opportunity arose to chase after Cape grey mongoose – but understandably she refused to walk with me where the rogue dog had almost seized her. We never again went near that place together.

In 2018 several of my friends and colleagues died. Two days after I prevented the dog attack, the first passed away. This was 'Mad' Mike Penman. Mike was one of the world's most extraordinary safari guides. He was also a cameraman and star of the hit Discovery Channel show *Mad Mike and Mark*, which had been viewed weekly in millions of people's homes worldwide. A few years older than me, Mike passed away peacefully in his sleep at the age of fifty-nine.

To me Mike was a kindred lion person, and I greatly admired his insights into animal behaviour. The year before Mike had played a prank on me on the phone. In a disguised African-accented voice he claimed that he was a safari lodge employee exposing captive elephant cruelty and he wanted me to testify urgently in court as an expert witness in the case. After stringing me along for many minutes (with me getting increasingly uptight), the voice I was listening to changed, and the caller said, 'Don't worry, Gareth, it is only me, Mike, Mike Penman!' The bugger.

The following month, my and Tuli's friend and neighbour Martin, who had gone through the 2017 fires with us, passed away. Then, in the same month, news reached me that my and George Adamson's friend Professor Brahmachary, brilliant biochemist and conservationist who had undertaken tiger behavioural studies for half a century, passed away at the age of eighty-six. 'Brahm', as he preferred to be called and I spent weeks together at George's camp in the Kora National Reserve. Of Brahm I had written in my book, *The Lions' Legacy:*

Just after my return (to Kora), I witnessed the arrival of Professor Brahmachary from Calcutta, India. Brahm as we called him is one of the most delightful and interesting men I have ever had the privilege of meeting. He is a small man with a flamboyant lecturer's manner, who when answering questions about his work, marches up and down, emphasizing an important point with a suddenly out thrust hand ... We had the most entertaining evenings, with Brahm prompting many tales from George, and often correcting and prompting him if he had forgotten a detail, name or place.

Also in February American conservationist Esmond Bradley Martin died. He was the world's foremost researcher and expert on the illegal trade in elephant ivory. He was murdered at his home in Nairobi, Kenya.

Two months later my friend Daphne Sheldrick passed away at the age of eighty-three. Daphne was simply a wildlife legend. For over thirty years she and her David Sheldrick Wildlife Trust team rescued, raised and rehabilitated over one hundred elephant orphans back into the wilds. In 2009 Daphne kindly wrote the Foreword to *The Secret Elephants*, stating:

> ... and I hope his moving narrative will ensure that the Knysna elephants are viewed with wonder and awe as a national and international treasure, symbolic of endurance against all odds, as well as symbolic of the precarious nature of their beleaguered species.

Also in April my colleague Louise Joubert, founder of the Sanwild Wildlife Sanctuary, was tragically killed in a car accident. She was fifty-nine.

Two months later, in July, Tuli was diagnosed with tumours on her liver and spleen and two weeks later I had to put her down. I had lost my loyal companion of almost a decade. In all that time, we were only ever apart for a few days at a time. After she passed away, I began to walk less and less into the haunts where we had searched for signs of the otang. It was too painful to be out there without Tuli.

On the evening that Tuli was diagnosed at the local veterinary clinic, my good friend Thembela drove us home, and an extraordinary encounter with an otang took place on the way – but I was not to know about it until one week later.

Thembela is a young Xhosa conservationist who, with his team, works in conjunction with SANParks in undertaking the removal of alien trees. Thembela has always been fascinated by my work on the Knysna elephants, whose range he and his team work in with the alien tree removal programme. He has read several of my books, and whenever we meet up we talk about the elephants.

Because his work entails being in places where the otang occurs, I told him one day about their existence. I did this partly to prepare him for the shock should he see one, and partly to ask him if any members of his team had seen or heard about the otang.

A week after Tuli's diagnosis, Thembela and I were driving back to the cabin from Knysna when he suddenly turned to me and asked, 'Gareth, the otang, are there smaller ones too?' Surprised by his question, I replied, 'Of course, Thembela, they are just like people. Why do you ask?' 'Because,' he replied, 'that night we were bringing Tuli back from the vet's, a small otang ran across the road as I slowed to go over that speed bump alongside the Salt River. You would not have seen it as you were facing backwards, comforting Tuli on the back seat. It was approximately one point two metres tall and dashed down from the right, and crossed the road in three quick strides. It was close and I saw it clearly in the headlights as I slowed to drive over the speed bump.'

Flabbergasted, I said to Thembela, 'Why did you not tell me about this at the time?' To which he gave me the typical otang witness reply, 'I thought you would not believe me, and I was shocked at seeing it. In fact I still feel a bit shocked.' With a smile I said to him, 'If anyone was to believe you, it would be me. After all, it was I who told you about the existence of the otang in the first place!'.

Thembela went on to tell me that the otang was reddish-brown in colour and well-proportioned and that he was astonished at the speed with which it moved. It had been only ten metres or so in front of the vehicle. It was a remarkable sighting, and knowing that Thembela is a most sincere person I have absolutely no doubt that he saw what he described to me.

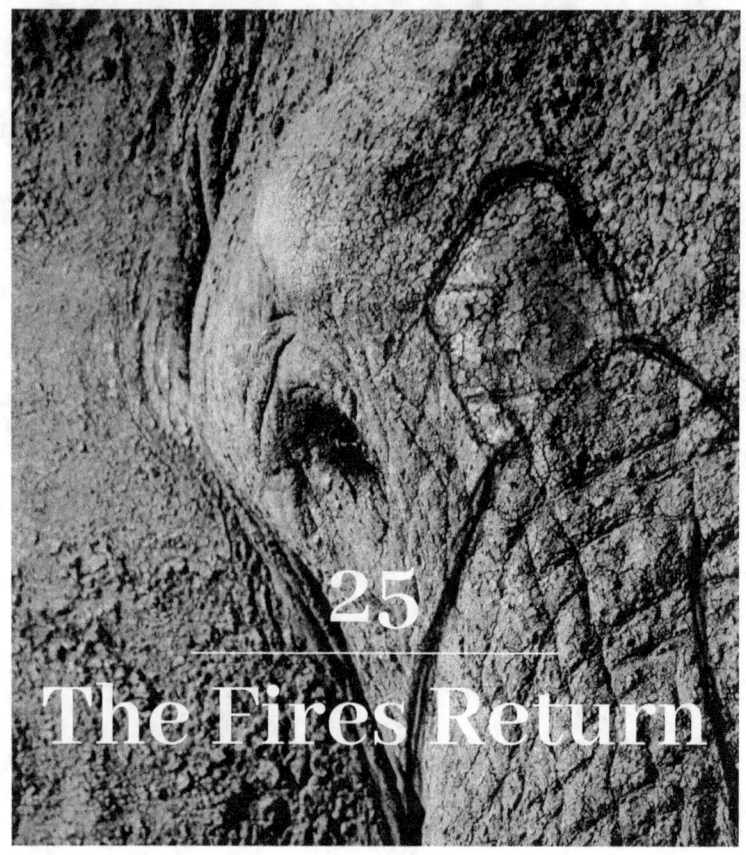

25
The Fires Return

On Sunday 21 October in the year of death, I was almost killed. The fact that I was not, in hindsight, indicated that I still had work to do – part of which was clearly the writing of this book.

It was a beautiful morning and, putting aside my sadness about Tuli not being with me, I set out with my rucksack on my back to do some exploring in our old haunts.

Every night during the past week I had woken up shouting because of nightmares about a man who was trying to kill me. I know now these were prophetic dreams.

As I was returning home from my explorations and about two

kilometres from the cabin, I heard a movement in the vegetation to my right. Thinking it might be a bushbuck, I stepped a couple of paces into the trees but seeing nothing I stepped back onto the track and continued on my way.

Then it happened, and all very quickly. Instinct warned me that something was behind me. I spun around, shouting loudly and saw a man just behind me, his arm raised above his head and a knife in his hand. I slammed into him.

My instinctive shouting and slamming into him no doubt saved my life, but now the fight began. He lunged at me repeatedly with the knife, yelling, 'I am going to kill you!' – but I saw fear in his eyes. We tussled on the ground. Then we both scrambled to our feet. I pulled an electric stun gun from my pocket – but it was useless. One has to be close to someone to use one of those – and you do not want to be close to someone with a knife.

At some point the stun gun fell to the ground and again we tussled on the ground. It was a gridlock for a while before he wriggled loose and ran away, grabbing my fallen rucksack as he went.

I picked up my stun gun and began heading homewards along the track. After about 200 metres I saw that I was bleeding. I had been stabbed.

Back in the bathroom at the cabin I began to clean the stab wounds very thoroughly. There were seven of them on my arms and legs and one on my head.

Never before had such an incident occurred in the area where I live, and I pray that nothing like it will ever happen again. Almost a year has passed now since the attack and the scars have faded.

A few days after I was attacked huge wildfires broke out in the mountains to the west. Tragically, well-known and well-liked veteran firefighting helicopter pilot Nico Heyns died when the Huey helicopter he was flying crashed. Nico had piloted a helicopter for the aerial scenes in our documentary *The Search for the Knysna Elephants*. His death was terrible news for all who had known him.

Lightning strikes combined with high temperatures (forty degrees was recorded in Knysna just prior to the wildfires, which was almost unheard of) and hurricane force winds ignited more than six sweeping fires, resulting in more than 200 000 hectares of mountain fynbos and forestry plantations burning. Some 1 500 people were displaced and, most tragically, the inferno claimed the lives of eight people, two women and six children, at a SANParks forest village. The horror of their deaths still haunts me.

Sixteen months before, when we experienced the earlier wildfires, I do not think that anyone could possibly have imagined that the area would be impacted by fire again so soon. Back then, it was 20 000 hectares of mostly coastal areas that burnt, demolishing human infrastructure. The October/November 2018 fires were overwhelmingly mountain wildfires. The mountain fynbos was old and tall (in places some eleven to twelve feet tall), and as it had not burnt for some three decades, it contained a high content of fuel, and therefore burnt extremely hot.

Ecologically the mountain wildfires were beneficial, with fire playing an important role in the germination of fynbos. Once again, as with the 2017 fires, the central indigenous forest did not burn, apart from the edges. But unlike the 2017 fires, the 2018 mountain wildfires caused me to have some concern for the elephants, and especially for the otang. Both species range into and are dependent on the mountain fynbos areas – and the elephants' entire mountain fynbos food source had been burnt to the ground.

I was fairly confident, though, that the elephants would have sought refuge from the mountain wildfires by moving south into the central forests (and I dearly hoped the otang would have done the same), but I could not determine this until 10 November when firefighting mopping-up operations were taking place and I could go out into the forest to search for them.

I headed out that Saturday morning with my colleague Owen Williams, founder of the NPO Hope for the Honeybees project (supported by the Gift of the Givers), and his friend Christa le Roux. Below the burnt Jonkersberg Mountain, in the luxuriant, green and wet forest (rain had fallen two days previously) to our absolute joy, we came across signs of two elephants that were moving together. Their footprints were smudged in a large muddy puddle. The elephants had moved south ahead of the fires. On the forest track we found droppings and abundant feeding signs. They had fed peacefully on the track in the forest as the fires raged in the north. They had been there a week before, and from the tracks, they had headed even deeper south into the cool wet forest. They were safe.

I think the three of us could have wept at finding signs of the elephants.

From the hind foot track measurements the two were the young (seventeen to eighteen year old) female and the twenty-five to thirty year old bull. Three days later on 13 November, while conducting one of my *Secret Elephants Forest Experiences* with guests, I found their tracks again, even further south in the forest, and I also found the tracks of a third elephant that was moving alone. Based on this evidence, I was fairly confident that the other elephants would have found safety and sanctuary in the forests.

But what of the otang? With the extreme infrequency of my sightings, or even that of tracks, it was almost impossible to determine what might have happened to them. In eighteen years I had only six sightings and found tracks (some of which I was not even certain were otang) perhaps a couple of dozen times. Unlike the elephants, who I can usually find signs of when I want to with some degree of certainty, I simply cannot do this with the otang.

The odds were that they did what the elephants did, and headed into the forest in advance of the wildfires, but not knowing this for certain was (and still is) extremely worrying.

What they might have endured in the mountain wildfires continues to haunt me as I write this.

I find myself pushing such thoughts from my mind.

Postscript

On the Edge of the Knysna Forest, August 2022

Almost immediately after this book was first published in 2020, further first-hand accounts of the otang were to be revealed to me.

The Knysna launch of *Beyond the Secret Elephants* was held at the town's main book shop, and in the capacity-filled venue, I gave a presentation to the audience about the otang and told of some of my experiences that are recounted in the book.

It was the first time that I had spoken publicly about these beings.

Many of the people in the audience that evening had no doubt either read or knew about my previous book, *The Secret Elephants*, in which I told how I rediscovered and studied the almost legendary Knysna elephants. Therefore, some of the audience might have naturally assumed that this new book was an update on my elephant research.

As I spoke about my and other people's accounts of the otang, I saw the audience was becoming increasingly engrossed in what I was talking about.

Earlier that evening, just before the book launch, my Xhosa friend Thembela, who one night in 2018 had seen an otang run in front of his car as he was driving my dog Tuli and me home after a visit to the local vet (as told in Chapter Twenty-Four), mentioned to me that he would be happy to recount those events to the audience. This was brave of him, and it was probably his way of embracing the occasion to shrug away the fears of ridicule that otang eyewitnesses so often feel.

After my presentation, Thembela was handed the microphone and, to a now very attentive audience, he told his astounding story (this was captured on video, and can be viewed at the following YouTube channel - https://www.tourismtattler.com/articles/reviews/beyond-the-secret-elephants/78696).

Movingly, at the story's end, and as Thembela thanked the audience for listening, spontaneous and hearty applause filled the book shop.

It was after Thembela's short presentation (and perhaps because of it, thus enabling people to let go of their own fears of ridicule) that people approached me and told of their own experiences.

This unfolded as I signed copies of the book.

Amongst the very first people in the queue lining up to have their copies signed, was a lady in her mid-thirties. She introduced herself and as she handed me her book she said, 'Thank you Gareth. Gosh, I thought I was coming to a book launch about the Knysna elephants. I had no idea it was going to be about these beings as well'.

As I was signing the book, she said, speaking softer, 'I saw one too, about twenty-two years ago when I was a teenager'.

Doubtless I looked up at her astounded.

I said, 'That is amazing. Where did this happen?'

And she told me. The encounter had occurred close to where my partner Kirsten and I live, on the very same road where in 2007 my friend Domi saw an otang dash across in front of her car's headlights (as I recounted in Chapter Fourteen).

A few days after the book launch, the lady kindly wrote me a full and detailed description of what had taken place on that road all those years before, and just a few months ago, she, with Kirsten and myself, went to the area where the encounter had taken place to in part re-enact, and analyse what had occurred.

Returning to the book launch, later as I was signing a book for a middle-aged lady, she quite suddenly said to me, 'My son saw one Gareth'.

I looked up from the book I had been signing.

'It happened a few years ago', the lady continued. 'He never told a soul, not even his wife, until he finally told me. He does not want me to talk about it though, so I will tell no more. Sorry, Gareth.'

About five minutes later a lady told me about an otang encounter a friend of hers had had, after which a well-known fine artist and palaeontology researcher and his journalist wife (who is a colleague of mine) approached me to sign his previously purchased, and already-read copy of the book.

As I signed the book, he said, 'I really enjoyed the book Gareth. I finished it the other day. Congratulations. It was brave of you to write it'.

I thanked him, and he nodded thoughtfully.

He then said, 'I think you have discovered a new hominoid species'.

After a brief pause, he added, 'My son had a sighting when he was about nine years old. The sighting has never left him'.

A week or so after the book launch the man's son, today a grown man, emailed to me his detailed account of what he had seen those years before as a child.

And as I write, I continue to receive eyewitness otang reports – and not just from the Knysna area, but from other areas in South Africa (and beyond).

A dear lady in her eighties whom I have known over the years emailed me one day after reading *Beyond the Secret Elephants* and described an encounter she and her parents had sixty years previously on a mountain pass some four hundred kilometres west of Knysna.

In all those long years she had barely told a soul about the encounter.

Another lady in her eighties also contacted me. Some fifty years previously she and her aunt had an encounter with two otangs near a small town in the foothills of the Maluti Mountains, many hundreds of kilometres north of Knysna.

She had initially told family and friends about the encounter, but after receiving teasing and banter, she spoke of it no more, until she read *Beyond the Secret Elephants* and contacted me.

Just last week I received a report from a gentleman who, in the mid-1960s saw an otang close to Knysna when he was a passenger in a Volkswagen Combi. He had a clear sighting, and he described the otang as being taller than the average man and that it was covered in dark hair. The man, like the two ladies, had barely mentioned the encounter to anyone since, until he finally contacted me.

Kirsten and I continue with our non-invasive otang research (and I also continue with my watchdog role for the Knysna elephants to maintain that they too are left undisturbed).

My most recent otang sighting occurred last year (2021) on the 18th of December. As part of our overall field research, we have embarked upon a bioacoustics project, recording with a digital recorder. We leave the recorder at specific places overnight and later review the recordings. To date, we have recorded the territorial calls of leopard, alarm calls of baboon and bushbuck, sounds of what might be that of feeding elephants, as well as the calls of various frog species, and the calls of nocturnal birds such as owls and nightjars.

On the day of the 18th December 2021 otang sighting, we had set up the recorder in an opening upon a ridge that overlooks the Knysna forest. It was late afternoon, with a light breeze coming from the southwest.

As we walked away from the opening upon the ridge, it was then that I thought I heard movement behind us. Ever since being stabbed by an attacker in our research area in 2018 (as I told of in Chapter Twenty-Five), I am hypervigilant whenever hearing sounds behind us when we are out in the field.

I swung around expecting to see a person, but there was no one. I stepped several meters towards the opening and scanned around.

It was then that I saw an otang.

Several seconds later, Kirsten stepped next to me, and I turned and said to her, 'I have just seen one'.

I did not have to tell her what I had seen. She instantly knew.

The otang had been standing in a gap, in what was otherwise a dense thicket of young trees. If it had been standing a foot to the left or a foot to the right, I would have not seen it.

Instead, it had been standing in the gap.

It was dark sooty grey in colour and was approximately five foot and eight inches in height. The details of the face were not clear, but it was standing looking directly in my direction.

If I had been able to see its eyes, we would have had direct eye contact.

I have absolutely no doubt that the otang had allowed itself to be seen.

Beyond the Secret Elephants - Audio File: Part 2

Acknowledgements

Many people have contributed, in a variety of ways, to my writing of *Beyond the Secret Elephants*. My thanks to:

Rozanne Savory, Kirsten Wohlfarth, Yvette van Wijk, my wonderful South African publisher Tracey McDonald, my fantastic editor Pam Thornley, Ian Redmond for kindly writing the Foreword to the book, Andreea 'Dudu' Elena Del Gaudio, Julie Carlisle, Wilfred Oraai, Karel Maswatie, Dominique Diane, Fransje van Riel, Dr Jeff Meldrum, Nicole Schafer, Joyce Poole, Trevor Carnaby, Lizette Moolman, Petra ten Velde, Venise Grossmann, Karin Saks, my brother Stewart, my cousin Andrew, my father Roger, Jim Parkes, Margaret Parkes, Louise de Bruin, Jo-Ann Bekker, Michael MacIver, Danie Baard, Karien Eigner, and Karl and Gudrun Bold.

My many thanks to Doug and Alex Hajicek of Hangar 1 Publishing for making this edition of the book possible.

Photographic Acknowledgements

Many thanks to the following for kindly allowing the use of your photographs in this book:

Dirk and Daniela Johnen (special thanks to Dirk for the front cover elephant photo), Fransje van Riel, Stewart Patterson, Christa le Roux, Arnaud de Groot, Wilfred Oraai, Dominique Diane, Mark van Wijk, Judith Von Prockl-Stadler, Kate Stephenson, and to Bydie Gottgens for the use of the photograph of Aftand, taken by her father Major Bruce Kinloch in 1968.

Copyright Acknowledgements

Many thanks to Dr Jeff Meldrum for allowing me to quote from his paper, 'Sasquatch & Other Wildmen: The Search for Relict Hominoids', *Journal of Scientific Exploration,* Vol. 30, No. 3, pp. 355-373, and to quote from the Foreword to his book, *Sasquatch: Legend Meets Science* (Forge Books, 2007). Thanks to Joyce Poole for allowing me to quote from her book, *Coming of Age with Elephants* (Hodder and Stoughton, 1996). Thanks too to Nicole Schafer for permission to quote from the abstract of her master's dissertation on her great documentary, *The Ballad of Rosalind Ballingall.* Also thanks to Carole Jahme for allowing me to quote from her excellent book, *Beauty and the Beasts: Woman, Ape and Evolution.* Virago Press (2001). And thank you to Massie & McQuilkin Literary Agents for kindly allowing me permission to reprint material from *Gorillas in the Mist* by Dian Fossey.

About the Author

Gareth Patterson is an award-winning environmentalist, wildlife researcher, public speaker, and author who is known internationally for his efforts to greater protect the lions and elephants of Africa. Born in England, he grew up in wild areas of western, eastern, and southern Africa. Several of his books about his life with lions and elephants have been published in many languages and editions. Gareth's work for Africa's wildlife has been featured in the media worldwide, as well as in international documentaries.

During the 2000s, Gareth rediscovered and studied the most southerly free-roaming elephants in the world: the highly endangered and elusive Knysna elephants of the southern Cape, South Africa. It was during this time that he became aware of the existence of mysterious relict hominoid beings known to the Knysna forest people as the 'Otang'.

Beyond the Secret Elephants is Gareth's twelfth book.

Get Social with Gareth

Websites

www.garethpatterson.com

www.sekaiafrica.com (Gareth's Sekai African Environmentalism Group)

Facebook

www.facebook.com/gareth.patterson.77

Publisher's Note

Visit www.hangar1publishing.com to learn more about the Author, and to stay up to date with our newest releases.

www.ingramcontent.com/pod-product-compliance
Lightning Source LLC
Chambersburg PA
CBHW061144120626
46546CB00005B/1924